Diehard Sins is of great h
encouragement to any lo
tian life. Rush Witt theologically and thoroughly deals with the
realities of sin's pervasive and destructive nature—but he doesn't
leave us hopeless. He supplies practical tools as a reminder that
although sin may be great, there are even greater, conquering
provisions found in Christ.

—**Jose Abella**, Lead Pastor, Providence Road Church, Miami,
    Florida

If you struggle with sin—which describes all of us—Rush has
provided great encouragement and help in *Diehard Sins*. Read it
and be encouraged to move forward with joy and renewed hope!

—**Amy Baker**, Certified Counselor, Association of Certified
    Biblical Counselors; Instructor and Counselor, Faith Bib-
    lical Counseling Ministries

Diehard Sins is written by a man who knows that we desperately
need vivid and memorable mental weapons to combat our deeply
rooted but hard-to-notice sins. While rightly reawakening the
reader to the dire problem of our "little" sins, Rush emphasizes
our hope in the gospel and offers more practical ways to meditate
on the gospel than any book I have read in a long time. Realistic
about both the slowness and the possibility of real growth in
fighting our sin patterns, *Diehard Sins* will repay the time you
invest with a rich harvest of ways to grow in daily godliness.

—**J. Alasdair Groves**, Director of Counseling, Christian
    Counseling and Educational Foundation New England

Long-developed patterns of sin die hard because sin is rooted
in the depths of our hearts. Christ alone offers hope! Rush
Witt serves the Christian church by offering wise, biblical, Christ-centered help for understanding and fighting the

seemingly "little" sins in our lives that threaten to quietly destroy us. *Diehard Sins* instructs, encourages, and challenges as Rush helps us to battle our persistent sins.

—**Johnny M. Hunt**, Senior Pastor, First Baptist Church, Woodstock, Georgia

In *Diehard Sins*, Rush demonstrates that God's revelation is practical. He helps readers to take up arms against our most buried and besetting sins. I most appreciate the way Rush encourages readers with the hope of biblical heart change—especially readers who are discouraged from wrestling with deep-rooted vices in their own strength. Not only will this book encourage you, but it will give you confidence in God's practical wisdom for fighting the sins that are hardest to kill.

—**Dale Johnson**, Executive Director, Association of Certified Biblical Counselors

Rush Witt has taken a great theological model used elsewhere for helping others and has applied it to personal growth. I love that he is helping us to wrestle with our identity in Christ, which redefines our persistent sin struggles. This book is both theological and practical.

—**Jason Lee**, Dean and Professor of Theological Studies, Cedarville University

Rush Witt has written a book that will be very helpful to those who read it and heed it. People who read and apply the biblically accurate and practical contents of the book will be greatly assisted in the process of sanctification—becoming more and more conformed to the image of Jesus Christ.

—**Wayne Mack**, Author, *A Fight to the Death: Taking Aim at Sin Within* and *God's Solutions to Life's Problems: Radical Change by the Power of God*

Christians are a people characterized by holiness. The Lord calls us to be holy as he is holy and commissions us to be separate from the world. Yet Christians also know that we daily fight indwelling sin. Rush Witt's *Diehard Sins* is a clarion call for holiness that also provides us with meaningful and theologically rich resources to fight indwelling sin. This book is a careful and refreshing resource that every Christian should read.

—**R. Albert Mohler Jr.**, President, The Southern Baptist Theological Seminary

Rush Witt addresses our most challenging sin struggles with practical biblical truth. He lays the theological foundation for understanding how progressive sanctification works and then builds a usable model for fighting sin and growing in grace. He draws from the wells of great Christian writers from the past while also offering helpful contemporary examples and illustrations. He speaks to the heart from a gospel-centered perspective. I personally benefited from reading this book and will commend it to the people I counsel and train.

—**Jim Newheiser**, Director of the Christian Counseling Program and Associate Professor of Christian Counseling and Practical Theology, Reformed Theological Seminary, Charlotte

Rush Witt has written a comprehensive book explaining the underlying foundation that Christians must have in order to fight the sin that remains in us. These are precious truths that every Christian needs to understand, know, and remember. It is obvious that Witt has a high view of God, and I highly recommend this book.

—**Martha Peace**, Biblical counselor, conference speaker, best-selling author

Your sins are hard to get rid of. They are diehard—they don't leave easily. They hang on, corrupting every part of you. If you need help fighting stubborn sins that don't ever seem to leave you alone, then this might be exactly the book you've been looking for.

—**Deepak Reju**, Pastor of Biblical Counseling and Family Ministry, Capitol Hill Baptist Church, Washington, DC

DIEHARD
SINS

DIEHARD SINS

How to Fight Wisely against
Destructive Daily Habits

RUSH WITT

P U B L I S H I N G

P.O. BOX 817 • PHILLIPSBURG • NEW JERSEY 08865-0817

Library of Congress Cataloging-in-Publication Data

Names: Witt, Rush, author.
Title: Diehard sins : how to fight wisely against destructive daily habits / Rush Witt.
Description: Phillipsburg : P&R Publishing, 2018. | Includes bibliographical
    references.
Identifiers: LCCN 2018023138| ISBN 9781629954851 (pbk.) | ISBN
    9781629954868 (epub) | ISBN 9781629954875 (mobi)
Subjects: LCSH: Habit breaking--Religious aspects--Christianity. | Sins. |
    Sin--Christianity.
Classification: LCC BV4598.7 .W58 2018 | DDC 241/.3--dc23
LC record available at https://lccn.loc.gov/2018023138

To my dear wife, Kathryn, and our five wonderful children.

"So then, brethren, we are under obligation,
not to the flesh, to live according to the flesh—
for if you are living according to the flesh, you must die;
but if by the Spirit you are putting to death the deeds
of the body, you will live" (Rom. 8:12–13).

I am delighted to kill sin with you,
my brothers and sisters in Christ,
until Christ gloriously comes again for us.

Contents

Foreword

I don't know how many people routinely read book forewords. I myself sometimes skip them in order to plunge right into the introduction. You won't offend me if you do the same. But if you're hesitating to read this book and need some preview and perspective, let me help you.

Why a book on *sin*? Because—despite myriads of theories by philosophers, sociologists, and psychologists—sin, in all its depth, remains the most fundamental explanation for human problems. I recall reading, many years ago, before heated gun-control debates or #MeToo movements, a newspaper article decrying our society's deterioration. The gist: with all the modern developments of our age, why can't we come up with a program to solve the problem of societal violence?

The Bible, of course, provides both the deepest diagnosis and the most profound cure for all who will heed its message. In this book, Dr. Rush Witt gives us a theologically sound, gospel-soaked treatment of sin and grace, lacing it with insightful quotes from various voices throughout church history. This is a safe book for you and for those you love.

So why *another* book on sin? I could list a half-dozen other solid evangelical treatments of this doctrine. But this one is different. Rush writes as a lead pastor who is on the ground with his people and as a trained biblical counselor who counsels

men and women in both his church and his community. With
the case wisdom of an active shepherd, he tells us (pseudo-
nymously) about Janet, Rob, Kristen, and others and about
their struggles to fight against their remaining sin.

Yet this book is not about sin in general but about a particular type—what the writer calls *diehard sins*. Don't think
about Bruce Willis. Think about your long-term, stubborn,
unyielding patterns of sin—not the biggies like murder or
adultery but the entrenched ones that don't lie down and die
quickly. Rush shows how these diehard sins manifest themselves in daily ways, dishonoring our Lord and debilitating our
Christian walk. Yet he also tells us how the active, saving work
of the Father, the Son, and the Holy Spirit brings real answers
to real people like Janet, you, and me.

But why another book on sin *by a writer you don't know?*
Because Dr. Rush Witt is worth knowing. I met Rush in 2004
when he served as an associate minister at Open Door Church
in Raleigh, North Carolina, and was completing his MDiv
degree at Southeastern Baptist Theological Seminary. As a new
professor at Southeastern, I joined Open Door and in time
became a part-time staff member with Rush. His biblical wisdom and relational skills were immediately evident. After Rush
graduated, the Lord called him to a pastoral staff position in
a large church in Florida. We reconnected when he became
one of my doctoral students in counseling at Southeastern and
then when our church sent him to plant the church he now
pastors in Columbus, Ohio. More recently I had the privilege
of supervising Rush through his certification process with the
Association of Certified Biblical Counselors, where his pastoral
wisdom again emerged.

It is my hope that this book will gain a wide readership—
not only among laypeople and those who pastor and counsel
them, but also among Bible college and seminary professors

who, like me, crave books that blend sound Bible doctrine with practical life application. With graduate training in both disciplines, and a heart that loves people, Rush models for us how to do this.

Robert D. Jones
Associate Professor of Biblical Counseling
The Southern Baptist Theological Seminary

Acknowledgments

As fallen people, we owe all that we are and do to God, who specially reveals truth to us. Above all else, we are heirs. There is no doubting that this book is the product of an enormous inheritance given to me by a myriad of spiritual benefactors. I am grateful for each of them.

With special gratitude I remember those who have made profound contributions to my life and doctrine. I give thanks for Dwayne Milioni and Robert Jones, two men who have taught, mentored, counseled, reproved, comforted, fathered, and befriended me in more ways than I could begin to count. More generally, I give thanks to God for the countless fellow believers who have faithfully modeled the Christian life for me in their writing, preaching, counseling, and day-to-day living.

I am also grateful for those who read, critiqued, edited, consulted, and encouraged my work. Thank you to my friends and colleagues at P&R Publishing, who have made *Diehard Sins* significantly better in every way.

Above all, I am grateful for my Redeemer God—Father, Son, and Holy Spirit—who showers infinite patience, grace, and love on diehard sinners like me.

Melody's Diehard Sin

"Blessed are the peacemakers." Melody has read those words a million times, yet she faces conflict on every side. Recently, Melody's one-year-old dachshund dug up the prized petunias of her neighbor, Joy. While Joy says that it's not a big deal and doesn't want Melody to replace them, it's obvious that she's nursing a grudge. Every time they lock eyes—as they're walking out to get the mail or toting the recyclables out on trash day—Melody can tell that all is not forgiven. But how to make peace, Melody doesn't know. So she fakes peace. Most of the time, she avoids Joy. Other times, she small-talks her way out of awkward exchanges.

Her relationship with Joy is not the only one that has suffered. Melody could make a long list of currently unresolved conflicts, and each one eats away at her. Why can't (or why won't) she make peace with others? In some cases, Melody has faked peace. In other cases, she has lashed out at her opponents. One thing is for sure: Melody is not the kind of peacemaker to whom Jesus promised His blessing.

INTRODUCTION

A Destructive Daily Problem

Living a just and holy life requires one to be capable of an objective and impartial evaluation of things.

ST. AUGUSTINE (354–430)

There is a giant problem in East Africa: snails. *Lissachatina fulica*, giant African land snails, originated in Kenya and have traversed as far as Asia and the Caribbean. They can wreak major havoc. In fact, in the United States it's illegal to possess one of these little critters. Illegal!!

Though they seem small and weak compared to other wildlife (at their adult height, they are slightly taller than a tennis ball),[1] these African snails live long, reproduce quickly, and perpetrate their evil work under the cover of darkness. Creeping in unnoticed, they devastate crops, forests, coastal areas, and cities. They also carry an insidious disease that is deadly to humans. In vain, hunters have levied against them all manner of quarantine, chemical warfare, and predatory creatures. Even flamethrowers were no use.

Diehard snails! How can such a small creature cause such a widespread problem? It takes only a little time and a little neglect.

1. "Giant African Snail," USDA APHIS, last modified June 4, 2018, https://www.aphis.usda.gov/aphis/ourfocus/planthealth/plant-pest-and-disease-programs/pests-and-diseases/giant-african-snail/ct_giant_african_snail_home.

Diehard Sins

This book is about sins. Not the ugly, notorious sins we have come to know and hate. But the little, daily sins. The snail-sized sin habits that slither undetected in the shadows, beneath a fire-resistant shell, and eat up our lives from the inside out. This book is about the sins that nag us, resist our spiritual treatments, and persist beyond all our measures to contain them. The subtle sins. The respectable and acceptable sins. The resilient and relentless sins. *The diehard sins.*

In spy novels, the silent assassin learns to live incognito, waiting and plotting his deadly deeds. Our sins can be very much like that. We hustle through life while they escape our notice and fester just beneath our noses. Either we don't recognize them as sins because they're commonplace in our lives or cultures, or we know that they're sinful but have given up on changing them. With the passage of time, we accept them as a disappointing, natural part of life. These sins are hard to fight because they are concealed from us.

Puritan pastor John Owen provides this ominous warning: "Be killing sin or it will be killing you."[2] For many Christians, the sins that "will be killing" us are not the million-dollar sins like murder or rape. We often have sufficient reason to avoid them. Rather, the hidden faults that fly under the radar—at the lower altitudes of our hearts—are the sins that cause us the most trouble. If we are not alert, we practice them day by day and they burrow into our lives like lice. And once they are settled in, extermination becomes all the more difficult.

I have known people with a deadly peanut allergy. Even a whiff of peanut butter constricts their airways and immediately endangers their lives. The most serious allergies don't

2. John Owen, *The Mortification of Sin: Dealing With Sin in Your Life* (1656; repr., Fearn, UK: Christian Focus, 1996), 28.

even allow the sufferer enough time to reach a doctor for help, meaning that the person must remain ever ready to jab himself with a shot of medicine in order to reverse the violent reaction. The fight against sin carries a similar quality. We depend on pastors, counselors, and other Christian friends to give us wise counsel. But we also need a growing ability to minister the Word of God to our own souls. Immeasurable hope and help await you as you learn to kill the diehard sins that plague you, because, no matter how deep your sin struggle runs, there is hope through Christ and His Word.

The Gift That Keeps on Giving

Newspapers of the 1920s offered readers "the gift that keeps on giving": the Victor Micro-synchronous Radio Console with Electrola. Happy families tuned in to the Victor-Radio every night, and their delight continued on and on. Although I was not aware of it at the time, the Lord gave my wife and me a gift much like this. (No, it wasn't a radio.) Two years into our marriage, during an exceptionally hard time, He called us to biblical counseling through the care of a faithful pastor.

Despite growing up in a faithful Christian family, my wife had walked a dark path. Amid life-dominating despair and recurring panic attacks, she had twice attempted suicide. She had been hospitalized in prominent psychiatric wards and had received nearly every psychiatric treatment available, including electro-convulsive therapy (an option of last resort). Soon after our marriage, we moved seven hundred miles from home in order to go to seminary—two broken people who were intimately acquainted, yet disappointed, with the full gamut of psychiatric help—and there we heard for the first time about the grace of Christ and the sufficiency of His Word for the care and cure of sinful, suffering souls like ours.

We were confused, amazed, and panicked all at once. This was very new to us. The next few weeks of class were especially eye-opening and challenging. We faced new truths about the nature of our persistent problems. These truths were hard to hear, and we didn't immediately respond well. But by God's grace we scraped together what little courage we had and reached out to the professor of the class for help: "We've never heard any of this before, and we really need to talk to you." He abounded with generosity and understanding. The next Friday we entered a simple yet life-changing season of gospel-centered, grace-driven biblical counseling.

There were good days and bad days. Sometimes the truth was a sweet salve for our souls; other times we spewed our medicine and stomped off in disgust. In small, hesitant steps, we found hope, help, and lasting biblical change. The colors of our world became brighter as God's truth renewed our minds. The fingers of depression and anxiety that had relentlessly gripped my dear wife (and me too at times) were pried away. The process of change was sometimes unpleasant and often slow—but, looking back, we wouldn't wish it any other way. Through it we received lasting benefits.

The transformation God worked in my wife and me through biblical counseling compelled me to discover ways to instill Christ-centered hope in the lives of others. With each step toward becoming more competent in the care of others, I became a more competent counselor of myself. The Scriptures rang true: all the trials and temptations addressed in my counseling were common to man—common even to me (see 1 Cor. 10:13). In every case, I gave the people who I counseled the same comprehensive counsel of God's Word that I myself needed. And I counseled myself in the same ways. The gift of biblical counseling that I received many years ago has kept on giving to me, helping me in my own walk with Christ.

The Three-Part Plan

My method of caring for others through counseling and discipleship is simple. When ministering to another person, I use a three-fold plan: enter his world, understand his need, and then bring Christ and His answers to the person.[3] It is by no means simplistic, but it is simple. As you will see in this book, I have adapted this method of ministry to others and presented it as a tool for fighting sin and caring for our own souls day by day. With practice, it has become second nature to me, and I hope it will become second nature to you too.

1. *Enter* with joy into your struggle against destructive daily habits,
2. *understand* your real needs in the fight, and then
3. *bring* Christ and His provisions to bear on your beliefs and desires.

The three steps of the plan are specifically drawn from Matthew 9:35–36, but they more broadly represent Jesus's entire ministry. In an unassuming passage of his gospel, Matthew gives a glimpse of Jesus's normal mode of ministry.

> Jesus was going through all the cities and villages, teaching in their synagogues and proclaiming the gospel of the kingdom, and healing every kind of disease and every kind of sickness. Seeing the people, He felt compassion for them, because they were distressed and dispirited like sheep without a shepherd. (Matt. 9:35–36)

---

3. I learned this approach to ministry from my mentor, Robert Jones. He applies it to counseling others; I am adapting it for personal growth. If you skipped over the foreword that he wrote for this book, please read it.

On a mission of love, Jesus *entered* our world by His incarnation and even walked our streets. He would actively traverse the cities and villages. Jesus routinely spent time with people and entered into the dark and difficult experiences of life. The Lord of glory did not remain in His regal, heavenly home; rather, He condescended into our fallen world—born in a manger, living in poverty, and working with His hands. Though sinless, He was tempted as we are and suffered a cruel atoning death. Many people may love me, but none would stoop down in such a magnificent way for me. Jesus entered my world and yours.

As one of us, Jesus *understands* our true needs. Every thoughtful person has some sense of our common spiritual problem. Every person knows that there is a God "with whom we have to do" (Heb. 4:13; see also Rom. 1:21). But the blinding influence of sin hides the true nature of our need from view. In the light of a doctor's knowledge, a patient's crude self-diagnosis falls flat. Our Great Physician understands our need. When Jesus went through the villages, He understood the people He encountered. He saw their sinful, distressed, and broken spirits. He saw sheep in need of a shepherd.

What is so impressive about a shepherd? A shepherd understands his sheep. As in Psalm 23, the divine Shepherd knows the whereabouts of His sheep, the dangers they face, the nourishment they lack, and the restoring care they need. The Lord understands the people into whose world He enters.

Not only that, Jesus *brings* His provisions and resources. By His perfect knowledge, understanding, and wisdom, He not only cared for people's broken, diseased bodies but also brought help for their souls. Jesus *counseled* the people who He met in the cities and villages. He taught them biblical truth in their synagogues, and He ministered the good news of His kingdom to their souls.

Ultimately, He brought the people *Himself.* In the synagogue or on the street corner or house-to-house, Jesus and His disciples didn't present a program or tool for changing lives. Jesus didn't create an app for fixing life problems. He brought Himself—His perfect person, His unstoppable power, His eternal promises and purposes. Jesus entered our world, understood our need, and brought to us His power and grace.

Preparing for the Fight

This book contains a mixture of theological and practical considerations for launching your grace-empowered fight against sin habits. Along the way, we will carefully consider the nature of sin, the issues of life, and how our Redeemer God— Father, Son, and Holy Spirit—relentlessly works in us to kill our relentless sins.

We all love pragmatic answers. My own natural inclination is to cut to the chase. *Just tell me what to do so I can get some relief.* But please resist the temptation to jump to the parts of the book that seem more practical. God has wisely scattered the treasures of sanctification across the entire field, from the hills of knowledge to the valleys of practice. Each chapter serves an integral role in sharpening your knowledge of and perspective on sin. Without the correct diagnosis, the effective remedy will never come.

Reflections for the Fight

1. What good and unending gifts has God given to you in Christ?
2. How have you counseled God's Word to others? In what ways do you need to grow stronger in this area?
3. What do you think it will mean for you to counsel yourself?

PART 1

Enter with Joy into Your
Struggle against Daily Sin

Eliza's Diehard Sin

Many people love a good story. Mystery. Suspense. Intrigue. Danger. What's not to love? Eliza eats it up with a spoon. But as she grows in her walk with Christ, she begins to notice her taste for real-life mystery, suspense, intrigue, and danger. She loves to hear the juicy news of her friends' latest breakups and the water-cooler whispers about who is moving up and who is moving out in her workplace. The stories make her adrenaline surge. She is addicted to the rumor mill.

Eventually, a close Christian friend gently confronts Eliza about her participation in these corner conversations. She agrees with her friend and makes a commitment to change. But no matter what she tries, her heart is drawn in like a mosquito to a hypnotic buzzing strobe. As she struggles to break free from her addiction to gab, she quickly realizes that this seemingly innocent sin will die hard, if it will die at all.

1

The DNA of Sin

*Sins are many times hid from the godly man's eye, though he
commits them, because he is not diligent and accurate in making
a search of himself, and in an impartial studying of his own ways.*

ANTHONY BURGESS (1600–1663)

In 1882, beneath the majestic Sudety Mountains, a child
named Gregor was born—the only son of Anton and Rosine
Mendel. An Austrian farm boy, Gregor grew to love the created world of God's creatures. He cultivated the family garden
and nurtured their bee collection. These experiences led him
to pursue a higher education in the sciences. But financial
troubles put a damper on his school plans. In his twenties,
Gregor became a friar in the Augustinian order of monks,
preferring the monastic offer of freedom from anxiety (and
the free tuition)! Although he studied for only a brief period
of time, Gregor's scientific exploration led to an invaluable
discovery: DNA.

Biologists had known about the inheritance of traits passed
down through the generations. But they knew little else about
it until Gregor, the father of genetics, began to unlock a hidden
reality through his work with pea plants. Over the following
century, efforts to crack the vault of genetic codes led Watson
and Crick to discover the foundations of organic life. Standing

on the shoulders of Mendel and others, Watson and Crick formalized the double-helix model of DNA, which made the molecular sciences all the more useful. Since 1953, DNA has played a regular part in the evening news, crime scene investigations, ancestry research, disease prevention, and more. What took so long for someone to finally look beneath the surface and find the DNA?

I often ask this same question of myself: What took you so long, Rush? I've been slow to understand the most important truths of life. I came to Christ a little later than some, it's true. But even then, for the first ten years of my walk with Christ, I was nearly oblivious to the important and powerful realities at work beneath my skin, in hidden recesses of my heart. Regrettably, it wasn't until much later that my eyes were clearly opened to consider the root of life's struggles: my pervasive, controlling sin nature.

Sins are hard to detect and kill because they are engrained in us. Like a method actor inhabiting his character, sin meshes with our souls. It is inside our hearts, insidiously interacting with every aspect of our being and exerting a measure of power over us.[1] The Christian must wage a personal war of epic proportions and constant conflict against sin. If we are to gain any victory against it, we must understand its DNA. That knowledge will help us to develop a battle plan through which we can form a God-centered and effective response to ongoing sin.

---

1. Paul describes this conflict in Romans 7. He knows what is good and right—he wants to please God—but he fails to carry it out. Sin is at work against Paul, tripping up his pursuit of godliness: "The good that I want, I do not do, but I practice the very evil that I do not want. . . . I joyfully concur with the law of God in the inner man, but I see a different law in the members of my body, waging war against the law of my mind and making me a prisoner of the law of sin which is in my members" (v. 19, 22–23).

What Is Sin?

If someone asked you to answer this question, what would you say? How do you define something that is unseen, sinister, deceitful, and malicious all at the same time? Even if you come to a sincere definition, how do you know that your own sin hasn't thrown you off the scent trail? To know what sin is, we need a reliable source of truth that is unaffected by the ravages of sin. In the special revelation of God's Word, and in God's Son, we have what we need. As the Word of Christ dwells in our hearts, we know the truth about sin.

Sin Commits a Lawless Act

The Bible speaks of sin as an act that transgresses God's law. Every time that we sin, in a big or small way, we violate a commandment, rule, or precept that God has established for us. "Everyone who practices sin also practices lawlessness; and sin is lawlessness," says John (1 John 3:4). The Westminster Shorter Catechism defines sin as "any want of conformity unto, or transgression of, the law of God."[2]

The laws of God were revealed to His people in the Old Testament and the New Testament—in part as a way of life. His laws are good, and they keep us on His straight and narrow path. When obeyed, they have a powerful ability to hem us in and even restrain our sinful inclinations (see Prov. 29:18). But, through sin, God's law is broken, placing us in danger of appropriate consequences and discipline from our heavenly Father. Owning our sins as serious transgressions of God's precepts alerts us to when and how we have gone astray. God's laws in Scripture are objective and easy to identify.

---

2. Westminster Shorter Catechism, answer 14.

Sin Presents a Rebellious Attitude

Scripture also depicts sin as the violation of God's will. Since God's commands were given according to His revealed plans for us, all sin involves a rebellious attitude against the Lawgiver. Paul wrote this caution to the Ephesian Christians:

> Therefore be careful how you walk, not as unwise men but as wise, making the most of your time, because the days are evil. So then do not be foolish, but understand what the will of the Lord is. (Eph. 5:15–17)

Instead of allowing our sin to persist, we must learn God's will, and from there we will know how to change. Do you think of your sins as violations of God's wishes and desires?

In the Bible, God urges us to live our lives according to His will. Sin says, "No. I prefer my will over yours. I'll go my way." Sin is, therefore, never merely a matter of rule breaking. The words of pastor R.C. Sproul remind us that "sin is cosmic treason. Sin is treason against a perfectly pure Sovereign. It is an act of supreme ingratitude toward the One to whom we owe everything, to the One who has given us life itself."[3]

Sin also alerts us to what we could describe as *disordered affections*—failure to love and worship God from the heart. One of the church fathers named Augustine taught that right living involves the ability to recognize when our hearts go wrong—when we are loving what we should not love.[4] A goal of our conflict with sin is not that we would be better rule-followers, but that we would be more faithful Christ-lovers. This means that sin is not only an obedience problem but a worship disorder too.

But that's not all.

---

3. R.C. Sproul, *The Holiness of God* (Carol Stream, IL: Tyndale, 1985), 115.
4. See his quote on the subject at the beginning of appendix D, on page 199.

Sin Displays an Ungodly Attribute

Sin is the fundamental distortion of our likeness to God's holy character. Whenever we sin, we also fail to think, act, feel, or talk like our Creator. Children tend to favor the appearance of their parents. When there is a strong likeness between them, the children are said to be the spitting image of their parents. This cliché could be applied to our created likeness to our Creator. Simply put, God created image-bearers who could reflect His glory and display His character. We exist in order to image Him, but sin holds us back and perverts the portrait we would like to project.

Alarms should ring when we think about our sin as a whole and when we notice the various sin habits that we wish would die already. We may feel an overwhelming sense of despair. But we shouldn't give up in our contemplation of sin. By grace, we can rejoice, in the words of David,

> How blessed is he whose transgression is forgiven,
> Whose sin is covered!
> How blessed is the man to whom the LORD does not impute
> iniquity,
> And in whose spirit there is no deceit! (Ps. 32:1–2)

We have abundant hope in the face of our sin.

Where Did It Come From?

God is perfect, and the Bible tells us that He didn't create sin in human beings. Rather, God created us good and in His image. He created us in true righteousness and holiness, so we might know Him, love Him, and live with Him happily ever after.[5] So then, from where did our sinful nature come?

---

5. See the Heidelberg Catechism, answer 6.

The Bible teaches that our sin originated with our first parents, Adam and Eve. In a paradise world, fashioned by the hand of God, the first humans chose their own way. Spiritual darkness fell, and the whole world became shrouded in the deadly curse of sin. Ever since then, each person in history (except for Jesus) was born with a sinful, fallen human nature. Like a delicate garment eaten through by moths, the perfect nature that God created in us decayed in a moment.

Original sin, as it is called, was subsequently passed down from generation to generation. And today, all our daily diehard sins spring from the original sin nature that lurks in us. Jesus graciously repairs the holes in our fallen human nature, as we are conformed to His image, until the day of final redemption. For now, sin remains, and we must struggle against it.

When you read the Genesis account of the fall of mankind into sin, you might be tempted to cast aspersions on Adam and Eve. During especially epic battles with sin, have you ever thought or said, "This is all their fault! Adam and Eve made me this way!"?

While it is true that Adam and Eve were the first to sin, we are wrong to shift the blame to them. They were our first parents as well as our representatives. We are not only guilty by association; we are truly, personally guilty of the fall. Adam's sin was imputed to all mankind. Therefore, from the moment of our conception—before any of us actually sinned on our own—we were sinners in need of God's saving and transforming grace (see Rom. 5:12–14).

This may be a new, frightening, and even despairing thought. Just hold on, because I have more good news for you. Paul proclaims the hope of redemption for sinners like us when he writes, "If by the transgression of the one [i.e., Adam] the many died, much more did the grace of God and the gift by the grace of the one Man, Jesus Christ, abound to the many"

(Rom. 5:15). Just as sin came to us through the first Adam, perfect righteousness comes to us through faith in the second Adam, Jesus Christ. Through His life, death, and resurrection, Jesus has assured the end of sin's reign. Therefore, we who fight hard against sin—even the sins that fight hardest against us—do not lose hope. The light of Christ's glory and grace shines at the end of this dark tunnel.

Where Does It Lead?

If we do not take sin seriously, sins will manifest in two directions—toward God (upward) and toward people (outward). In some sense, every sinful fault is an upward sin—a failure to love God. The *New City Catechism* says, "Sin is rejecting or ignoring God in the world he created, rebelling against him by living without reference to him, not being or doing what he requires in his law—resulting in our death and the disintegration of all creation."[6] All sin is against our righteous and loving Creator. Yet some sins are more clearly directed against Him, while other sins are more clearly against our neighbors. This second category of sin is outward.

The Ten Commandments fall into two categories, loving God and loving our neighbor, and our many sins may be understood in this light. Look closely at the Decalogue (see Ex. 20:2–17). The first four commands are clearly upward. The following six commands are notably outward.

Upward Commands
1. You shall have no other gods before Me.
2. You shall not make for yourself an idol.

6. Kathy Keller, *The New City Catechism: 52 Questions and Answers for Our Hearts and Minds* (Wheaton, IL: Crossway, 2017), answer 16.

3. You shall not take the name of the LORD your God in vain.
4. Remember the Sabbath day, to keep it holy.

Outward Commands

5. Honor your father and your mother.
6. You shall not murder.
7. You shall not commit adultery.
8. You shall not steal.
9. You shall not bear false witness against your neighbor.
10. You shall not covet.

Think about your wrestlings with sin. Can you pinpoint sins that you commit on a daily basis that move either upward or outward? Can you identify specific ways that you dishonor God? Can you see other ways in which you fail people?

As one faithful pastor's writings convinced me, my heart is an idol factory—perpetually inventing new ways to sin against God and man.[7] And so is yours. Our fallen human nature boasts endless ways to churn out sinful habits, and in the process of committing some sins we spin off even more ways of sinning. To list all of them would take untold lifetimes. Yet we still must take an account if we are to make progress in this important spiritual fight.

Try crafting your own personal list. Thinking in terms of upward and outward sins will help you to take inventory of the battle you will face and, later, help you to respond wisely.

---

7. See John Calvin, *Institutes of the Christian Religion*, ed. John T. McNeill, trans. Ford Lewis Battles, vol. 1 (Louisville: Westminster John Knox Press, 1960), 1.11.8.

Where Is It Headed?

C. S. Lewis's *The Lion, the Witch, and the Wardrobe* paints a bleak and oppressive picture of the curse of sin. The hero, Aslan, is the king of Narnia. Aslan's domain is temporarily under the magical influence of the White Witch, whose spell has changed the once beautiful landscape into a place where it's "always winter and never Christmas." Despite the present darkness, Aslan maintains his sovereign rule and performs a renewing work. As he moves through the land, he melts the snow and instills new life across the frozen panorama. All the creatures of Narnia await his return, when he will finally and fully break the spell.

Scripture presents a real promise of life-changing renewal in Jesus Christ. Through His atoning work on our behalf, Jesus has secured for us a final victory over sin. Through faith in Him, we are granted a sure and complete salvation from the power and penalty of sin. In his letter to the Ephesians, Paul writes that God raised us up with Jesus and then seated us with Him in the heavenlies (see Eph. 2:6). Our final redemption is already complete. Yet here we are in the earthlies, wrestling with life day after day. In one sense, our destiny is set. In another sense, we are still on our way to our destination, working out our salvation according to God's power in us. Paul comforts us: "We do not lose heart, but though our outer man is decaying, yet our inner man is being renewed day by day" (2 Cor. 4:16). Where is sin headed? It is fading away, as God progressively renews us in this life.

God's process of renewal—which brings an end to sin— happens gradually over time. For most of us, the work of sanctification creeps along much more slowly than we would like. Perhaps the lumbering pace of spiritual growth has provoked your attention to the presence of the diehard sins that are discussed in this book.

This is what happened to Eliza. Untangling herself from the tentacles of gossip would not come easily or without a fight. For Eliza, and for many of us, change happens slowly. Regardless of how fast your problems change, you may rest assured in the confidence that "He who began a good work in you will perfect it until the day of Christ Jesus" (Phil. 1:6). We can participate joyfully in this war because there is hope, even when the battles rage on longer than we think they should. Our sin is going somewhere. It's going away . . . but it's not going away without a serious, searching fight.

What Can Be Done about It Now?

If our fall into sin had been avoided, present-day Christians would live a life of continual peace without the slightest conflict, temptation, trial, or trouble. As redeemed kingdom citizens sojourning in a foreign and fallen land, we live with Christ, war against sin, and deny self. If we fail to employ the weapons of our faith or to follow our Captain into the battle, we will surely languish. We will be like soldiers who forget the war is raging, who mistake the intense sounds of combat for thunder booming in the distance.

Regrettably, some Christians live as though our enemy has lulled them to sleep—their impervious heads resting quietly on pillows of blind contentment. They feel no pressure to make war with sin. Their lives get along well without much fuss needed over the world, the flesh, or the devil—that is, until the arrows of sin pierce the pleasant facade they have come to enjoy. By God's grace, the sting of sin arouses us to take up spiritual weapons and fight back.

Gaining control over our sin struggles requires a wartime mentality. But this war is unique. It is a dependent, grace-fought war. Our dependence is on God, who helps us by His grace. He gave us His Son and His Word to strengthen us in the fray. For this reason the Scriptures say,

> The word of God is living and active and sharper than any two-edged sword . . . and able to judge the thoughts and intentions of the heart. . . . We do not have a high priest who cannot sympathize with our weaknesses, but One who has been tempted in all things as we are, yet without sin. Therefore let us draw near with confidence to the throne of grace, so that we may receive mercy and find grace to help in time of need. (Heb. 4:12, 15–16)

These gifts of His grace (and many more) embolden us to take action against sin—even the diehard sins of life. But just as the war of faith is a specific kind of war, the action that we take is a specific kind of action. I fear that we so easily fall back into the trap of believing that our battle is one of simple repentance and willpower. *Try harder. Change your ways. Do better.* These are the familiar mantras of modern self-help. But this is not the Christian way. All our multiplied self-efforts could never unleash enough firepower to preclude our diehard sins from ruling over us. We need the divine power of God, who wisely gives us particular tactics for the fight.

Jesus said that a wise king does not rush into battle but first surveys the situation, evaluating how the battle will be won. Don't rush into battle quite yet. There is more to examine about the nature of sin in the next chapter.

Reflections for the Fight

1. Why is understanding the DNA of sin an important part of addressing sin?
2. How does knowing the origin of sin in history help you find sin in the present?
3. Spend time meditating on the two Adams who are found in Romans 5. How are they different and similar? How is Jesus the better Adam?

Carl's Diehard Sin

Full-time pay for part-time hours. This is the kind of job that Carl hopes to get when he graduates from college next semester. The only thing bigger than Carl's chutzpah is his penchant for laziness. He sleeps in, procrastinates, cuts corners, and always is ready to fire off an excuse. He is what the Bible calls slothful. It's not that Carl is a recluse or is unmotivated. He is quite social and will put in many hours of work on the things he enjoys most. But when it comes to completing the more difficult tasks of adulthood or the less comfortable responsibilities that God has placed in his life, Carl's laziness kicks into overdrive.

To Carl, there is an art to laziness—he has a knack for talking his way out of responsibilities and assignments. What Carl cannot see is that he is unmotivated to do just about anything except completing his current pet project. Carl needs help. He needs someone who can get through to his heart and help him to unpack the web of beliefs and wants that hinder him from moving forward in various areas of life.

2

Hope for the Smoldering Cinder

*This violence for Heaven is the grand business of our
lives: what did we come into the world for else?*
THOMAS WATSON (1620–1686)

In the last chapter, we talked about the DNA of sin. But what
does sin look like in day-to-day life? You will see examples
in the stories of fellow sinners and sufferers that begin each
chapter of this book. Their sins aren't dramatic. They won't
make headlines in the church or in the world. They are, in fact,
the kind of small, respectable sins that nag at us relentlessly.
I see my reflection—one way or another—in every portrait.

These are what I am calling *diehard* sins, and we all need
God's help to face and overcome them. We are hindered, con-
founded, twisted, and turned by the sins that settle into our
hearts and latch onto our lives. These nagging, festering sins
can be just as dangerous and damaging as the presumptuous
sins that we dread the most. Yet these "smaller" sins often go
unnoticed and unaddressed. Like leeches left untreated, diehard sins swell with time—as do their impact on our spiritual
well-being. And even when we address them, diehard sins, by
their very definition, will not quickly or easily surrender.

Think of Carl. Though they love him, Carl's friends
were once quick to characterize him as lazy, indifferent, and

lackadaisical. Four years ago, he became persuaded of his need for change after failing two night classes that his employer required as part of maintaining his necessary certification. He sought out biblical counseling, and now his relationships are thriving and his improved work ethic has been rewarded with a promotion. However, Carl is daily tempted to pull back into his old, slothful way of life. He wonders whether the seductive desire for ease will ever finally fade.

I believe that every true follower of Christ has felt in some way what Carl feels: discouragement and even despair over their remaining sin. While we certainly can and should expect a measure of improvement when we practice spiritual disciplines, God—by His infinite, sovereign, and unsearchable wisdom—sees fit for sin to remain in some measure.[1] Even the godliest Christian men and women live with remaining sin. Beloved pastor and reformer John Calvin wrote, "The children of God are freed through regeneration from bondage to sin. Yet . . . there still remains in them a continuing occasion for struggle whereby they may be exercised; and not only be exercised, but also better learn their own weakness. . . . There remains in a regenerate man a smoldering cinder of evil, from which desires continually leap forth to allure and spur him to commit sin."[2]

Do you realize that sin remains in you today? Sin dies hard; it simply won't go away soon.

---

1. "During this life, this corruption of nature remains in those who are regenerated. Even though it is pardoned and put to death through Christ, yet both this corruption of nature and all actions arising from it are truly and actually sin" ("The Fall of Mankind, and Sin and Its Punishment," chapter 6 in "The 1689 Baptist Confession of Faith in Modern English," Founders Ministries, accessed July 20, 2018, https://founders.org/library/1689-confession/chapter-6-the-fall-of-mankind-and-sin-and-its-punishment/).

2. John Calvin, *Institutes of the Christian Religion*, ed. John T. McNeill, trans. Ford Lewis Battles, vol. 1 (Louisville: Westminster John Knox Press, 1960), 3.3.10.

Pushing Back the Fall

In July of 2004, we welcomed into the world our first little bundle of joy: a sweet baby girl with a full head of black hair. Eighteen months later, the Lord blessed us with another little girl . . . and then a boy, then another boy, then another girl. After five children, our quiver was full, and our home was bustling with mouths to feed. Parenthood brought into my life abounding marvels: the miracle of childbirth, the power of love at first sight, the speed at which helpless babies grow into young adulthood. Oh—and crumbs. To this day, I marvel at the sheer volume of food particles that fall from five little mouths onto the floor of every room in my house. We vacuum twice a day just to keep up.

With or without multiple children, those who keep a home understand the monotonous, mundane work of tidying up. It's never done. And once things are put in order, someone (or five someones) drags out the chaos again. It's a vicious cycle. But there is hope, because we know that we are dealing with a little corner of the fall.

Sweeping up crumbs daily is a simple picture of our war with diehard sins. Every morning, sin is there. And, every morning, we fight back with the divinely powerful weapons of God's grace. In fact, every effort that we make to live for the glory of God is, simultaneously, an effort that pushes back against the effects of sin in the world. The curse of sin is an adversary that we will not cease warring against until Christ comes to put His enemies under His feet. For now, God has willed that sin remain.

Why Fight Our Diehard Sins?

Why should we be concerned about our diehard sins if God has willed for them to remain? Our sovereign, wise, good

God is at work in the midst of and in spite of our sin. But this does not mean that the corrupt motives and affections within us are benign.

The Power of Temptation Remains

With sin comes temptation, and with temptation comes an occasion to either overcome or be overcome. "Temptation is like a knife, that may either cut the meat or the throat of a man; it may be his food or his poison, his exercise or his destruction," wrote John Owen.[3] Temptation's ultimate strength is not located in the tempter or his allurements. Temptation is fueled by the disposition of our hearts. If our hearts are open to sin, temptations succeed. If our hearts are set against sin, temptations fall flat.

Our High Priest, Jesus Christ, was tempted in all things but never sinned (see Heb. 4:15). Jesus's sinlessness is due not to a difference in the scheme of temptation but to a difference in the nature of His heart. Jesus lacked indwelling sin and, therefore, displayed immunity to the devil's advances. After forty days of temptations in the wilderness, Satan left Jesus until a more opportune time (see Luke 4:13). But, because of our remaining sin, now is *always* an opportune time for the devil to tempt us. It is always open season for temptation.

Has God left us to fend for ourselves, all alone in a raging sea of deadly temptations? Quite the contrary! By His sovereign power, He who rules over the wind and the waves rules over us. By His grace, He enables us to recognize and endure the temptations of this fallen world. Paul's words embolden us: "No temptation has overtaken you but such as is common to man; and God is faithful, who will not allow you to be

---

3. John Owen, "Of Temptation: The Nature and Power of It, Etc.," in William H. Goold, ed., *The Works of John Owen* (Edinburgh: T & T Clark, 1862), 6:92–93.

tempted beyond what you are able, but with the temptation will provide the way of escape also, so that you will be able to endure it" (1 Cor. 10:13). He is with us and keeping us and opening the way for us to growth and change, even through remaining sin and temptation. For this reason, we fight on.[4]

The Threat of Loss Remains

Sin is deadly. Our hope is secure in Christ, who has taken hold of us by grace through faith so that no one can snatch us away (see John 10:28). We are seated in the heavenly places with Christ (see Eph. 2:6). Indeed, nothing in all creation can separate us from the love of God in Christ (see Rom. 8:38–39). But, even so, sin is deadly. And with sin, a spiritual threat remains. We must act.

Has an unfamiliar sound ever startled you awake at night? You're sleeping soundly in the comfort of your own home when the floor creaks. Dazed, you hold your breath and tune your ears as your heart pounds in your throat. Are you dreaming? Is a prowler in the house? Is this a figment of your imagination? You're frozen under the covers.

What do you do next? You convince yourself that it's fine and drift back to sleep. In the morning, you rejoice that you were right and that all is well. But, as you wipe the sleep from your eyes, a question crosses your mind: What would you do in the presence of a credible nighttime threat?

Remaining sin presents a credible spiritual threat every day. Are you ready to respond? While salvation is secure in heaven for God's elect, sin threatens earthly losses. Failing to fight against sin can result in trouble at best and disaster at worst. Through the ministry of biblical counseling, I have seen

---

4. See Appendix B in order to learn a method for resisting temptation: Refuse—Replace—Pray—Praise.

the costly consequences of sin. One man sacrificed his business and drained $36,000 of his family's savings while binging on illegal drugs in a pay-by-hour motel room. Another counselee suffered the loss of his marriage and children through the sin of sexual infidelity. Still others have languished under the effects of another person's sinful choices. Hear again the seriousness in John Owen's words: "Do you mortify; do you make it your daily work; be always at it while you live; cease not a day from this work; be killing sin or it will be killing you."[5]

The Opposition to God's Glory Remains

The most important reason that we must fight against die-hard sin is for the glory of our gracious God. As long as sin remains, His fame and splendor are opposed. Nothing should trouble us more. God's glory is our hope. From all eternity, no feature of the universe is more valuable than the glory of God. David described God's glory as the ultimate object of all created reality: "The heavens are telling of the glory of God; and their expanse is declaring the work of His hands" (Ps. 19:1). Beyond all other afflictions produced by the fall, the offense to God's glory is supreme. Indeed, Jesus came into our world in order to display the splendor of God on the backdrop of sin, by destroying the works of the devil (see 1 John 3:8). And at the appointed future time, when He returns again to remove the curse forever, God's glory will shine forth without opposition.

On that blessed future day, we the righteous objects of Christ's grace will shine like the sun in the kingdom of our Father (see Matt. 13:43). Until then, we are ambassadors of the very glory of God. People who have been captivated by the

---

5. John Owen, *The Mortification of Sin* (1656; repr., London: Banner of Truth, 2004), 5.

unrivaled magnificence of God will have no higher aim than to magnify His glory.

We realize this incredible privilege and responsibility best when we treasure God as our highest affection. Pastor John Piper's life philosophy marks out well the path set before us: God is most glorified in us when we are most satisfied in Him. As long as we walk the earth, our attack on diehard sins must remain uniquely focused on maximizing God's glory.

Sin's Effect Is Not All That Remains

Diehard sin is alarming, but we need not despair. We know that sin remains because God has willed it to remain. He isn't worried or threatened. He isn't wringing His hands in heaven. He is finishing the unimaginable work that He began in eternity past. We need not shrink back in fear from diehard sin. The darkness of our hearts may not be eradicated in this life, but it will be "gradually removed by our growth in the knowledge of our Lord Jesus Christ."[6] God has drawn us to Himself, and in Christ we have begun a process of change. In His sovereignty, wisdom, and goodness, God has caused many gospel blessings to also remain.

Consider just four of these hope-filled gifts of God.

God's Presence Remains

To fight against diehard sin, we must remember that God has not left us alone in our fallen predicament to fend for ourselves. Like a faithful father who has compassion on his children, our heavenly Father has promised and purposed to stay with us. His abiding presence, in the midst of our struggle, is no small thing.

6. Owen, 6.

Since the genesis of mankind, God's transforming presence has given His people hope, help, and enabling grace in every time of need. During the exodus of Israel, Moses asked for assurance that the Lord would go with him as he led the people up toward the promised land, saying, "If Your presence does not go with us, do not lead us up from here. For how then can it be known that I have found favor in Your sight, I and Your people? Is it not by Your going with us, so that we, I and Your people, may be distinguished from all the other people who are upon the face of the earth?" (Ex. 33:15–16). The presence of the covenant God set Israel apart from all other nations. The elect people of God enjoyed His presence and the assurance of His favor. This is true today for every person who is in Christ. God is with us. His presence remains with us.

Our Dependence Remains

Since God's presence remains with us, our dependence on Him remains too. God uses the sin within us and our world to keep our eyes on Him continually.

How do you know whether someone is a Christian? By the words he uses or the creeds he confesses? Yes—but even an unbeliever can say some of the right things. By the works she does and the way she lives? Yes—but even the lost can accomplish some noble tasks. Beneath true confession and true life is a deep dependence on God. In a mysterious work of God's providence, He uses trials, troubles, temptations, and even our diehard sin to stir a Godward dependence in us. By His Spirit, God illumines our minds to the reality of remaining sin. As a result, we feel the deep, gnawing urge to be close to Him. We need Him to help us in the battle. If God did not open our eyes to this great spiritual need, our deceitful hearts would cast off all desire to be near Him.

When they were young, each of my children would draw

close to their mother or me the moment that they felt afraid. Children have a natural sense of dependence on their parents. In the face of persistent sin problems, we must thoroughly depend on the Lord.

When speaking of dependence on God, Jesus used the word *abide*: "I am the vine, you are the branches; he who abides in Me and I in him, he bears much fruit, for apart from Me you can do nothing" (John 15:5). Here the verb *abide* means to *remain with* Jesus. He is the nourishing vine, and we are His nourished branches. He has promised to remain with us despite our ongoing struggle with sin. And we must remain close to Him—we must depend on the Lord. If we don't abide with Him and He with us, we will fail to bear spiritual fruit. Our dependence remains.

God's Gospel Remains

The good news of Jesus Christ is our central weapon in the fight against diehard sins. Each and every one of the myriad truths and instructions revealed throughout the Bible draws its transformative power from the gospel. Unfortunately, there is much confusion among Christians today regarding the gospel. Some don't know what it is; others are unaware that the gospel is essential to every aspect of the Christian life. To wrestle effectively with the sin habits that plague us, we must know precisely what the gospel is all about.

The gospel is not about anything that you and I have done. It doesn't give us something to do. It doesn't tell us how to live. It's not a law or a list or a way of living life. The gospel is a heralded announcement about what Jesus Christ has done on behalf of sinners like us. It is the good news of God's Son, who entered our fallen world, became flesh, lived perfectly in our place, died sacrificially on the cross that we deserved, and triumphantly rose from the dead to raise us to life immortal.

From beginning to end, the gospel is about God and His determination to redeem a people for His own glory, in whom He will display the mighty power of His grace.

Therefore, our greatest hope for enduring and overcoming diehard sins is not based in our ability to perform or change. Our ultimate hope is in the God who has drawn us by His grace, spoken to us words of life, and promised to conform us to the image of His Son (see Rom. 8:29). Through the gospel, we have every means and every reason to remain at war with sin, no matter how bleak the outlook. The gospel remains.

Our Vigilance Remains

The Bible images the Christian life as a race, and we are to run it with endurance, "fixing our eyes on Jesus, the author and perfecter of faith, who for the joy set before Him endured the cross, despising the shame, and has sat down at the right hand of the throne of God" (Heb. 12:2). The Puritan Thomas Watson wrote, "In a race there's not only laying aside all weights that hinder, but a putting forth of all the strength of the body; a straining [of] every joint that men may press on with all swiftness to lay hold on the prize."[7] Are you running your race with endurance? Are your eyes set on Jesus, who began and will complete your journey of faith?

The Christian life is also imaged as a fight. Our life has a violent streak to it, as God enables us to do violence to our own fallen ways. We are to be like the boxer who strategically engages all his energies in order to defeat his opponent.

Paul wrote such striking words of war to his spiritual son, Timothy, challenging him to "fight the good fight of faith; take hold of the eternal life to which you were called, and you

---

7. Thomas Watson, *The Christian Soldier, or Heaven Taken by Storm* (New York, 1810), 68.

made the good confession in the presence of many witnesses"
(1 Tim. 6:12). Notice what strong language Paul uses to exhort
Timothy. He says to fight! It is not enough to be a diligent
student or a hard worker. We must be fighters—warriors even.
Timothy should be straining forward toward heaven, not resting lazily on earth.

The Christian life is a race to the finish and a faith-filled
fight against sin. Both metaphors express the need for discipline and focus. As in our day, ancient champions won races
and defeated opponents through concentrated self-control and
a purposeful training regimen.

> Run in such a way that you may win. Everyone who com-
> petes in the games exercises self-control in all things. They
> then do it to receive a perishable wreath, but we an imperish-
> able. Therefore I run in such a way, as not without aim; I box
> in such a way, as not beating the air; but I discipline my body
> and make it my slave, so that, after I have preached to others,
> I myself will not be disqualified. (1 Cor. 9:24–27)

All this adds up to a grand conclusion. We can with joy
and hope fight with vigilance against every hint of remaining
sin in our lives. God is with us, we are dependent on Him, and
by His good news we have the hope of sure victory in the end.

Responding to Diehard Sins

God calls us to be always *alert* to the reality of our diehard sin. "If we say that we have no sin, we are deceiving ourselves and the truth is not in us" (1 John 1:8). Countless wars
throughout history were lost because one side underestimated
the power of the enemy. For a similar spiritual reason, every follower of Christ should become a student of the doctrine of sin.

The apostle Peter cautioned his readers to be of sober spirit and on the alert (see 1 Peter 5:8). Do these words describe you? Are you watching your own heart, ready to enter the struggle and do gospel violence against the remaining sin habits in your life?

God also calls us to be always *repenting*. From Genesis to Revelation, the consistent response to sin is repentance—an inward act by which a person turns away from sin and toward God.[8] As a hiker tuned to his compass continually adjusts his course to true north, the Christian constantly turns back to God. The world, the flesh, and the devil seek to turn us from the narrow path, but by God's gracious provisions we steadily move in the direction of truth. The daily trouble of diehard sins calls us to maintain an attitude of repentance.

Finally, God calls us to be always *devoted* to Christ and His gospel. The Christian life is a constant succession of rehearsed truths. Christ greets us in the morning when we awake and His mercies are new (see Lam. 3:22–23). Christ lays our heads to rest every night. In every moment in between, we are comforted and empowered by the remembrance of His covenant love. Since we always need Christ, we must always be devoted to Him and always preaching the gospel to ourselves.

After expounding on the precious and magnificent promises of God, the apostle Peter wrote, "I will always be ready to remind you of these things, even though you already know them, and have been established in the truth which is present with you" (2 Peter 1:12). It may seem as though such an important response should come naturally to the people of God, but no. Sin has so polluted our hearts that living in the light of the gospel requires an intentional discipline of grace.

---

8. Louis Berkhof, *Systematic Theology*, new combined ed. (Grand Rapids: Eerdmans, 1996), 487.

Reflections for the Fight

1. How much thought have you given to the nature of your diehard sin?
2. Do you struggle to recognize your own diehard sins? If so, why? Is it that you don't easily see them as sinful? Or is it that you have tried and tried but in some ways have given up on seeing them changed?
3. In addition to God's presence, our dependence on Him, His gospel, and our vigilance in the fight, what other good gifts of God can you see remaining?
4. List three to five ways in which you need to strengthen your dependence on God. Are there certain areas of your life in which you need to depend on Him more?
5. Read 2 Peter 1:2–15. Notice how many times Peter emphasizes the importance of gospel reminders.
6. Turn to Appendix B. You will find a four-part method for maximizing the Word of God in your life. Start putting it into practice today.

Kristen's Diehard Sin

Of all her friends, Kristen is the loudest. She is spontaneous and opinionated, and this is what her friends love most about her. She is fun to be around and always good for a long, hearty laugh. But sometimes her jokes go a little too far. Doctors would say Kristen suffers from foot-in-mouth syndrome; in fact, it seems to her that the only time she opens her mouth is to change feet. By God's grace, she recognizes this problem and wants to see it changed. Her concern is growing as she realizes how hurtful her careless words are—and she senses a deeper problem. Frequently insensitive to other people, Kristen gives little thought to the consequences of her boisterous ways. She knows that replacing her insensitive words is important, but it will never be enough. The spontaneous and impulsive things that she says do not appear out of nowhere. They come from her heart, and her heart must change before she wakes up all alone.

3

The Art of Contented Discontent

Christ will not leave us till he has made us like himself, all glorious within and without, and presented us blameless before his Father.

RICHARD SIBBES (1577–1635)

God has the power to create the vast universe in six days. So why has He scheduled the standard baby for forty weeks of kicking feet and flailing elbows before breaking into the world? Why does it take so long? I can't know for sure, but I assume every pregnant woman has asked a question (or a thousand) like this one. During the last miserable days leading up to each of our children's due dates, my great-bellied wife became more and more like King David, who cried, "How long, O LORD? Will You forget me forever?" (Ps. 13:1). Long, sleepless, aching nights dragged into waddling, uncomfortable days. How long, O Lord—how long?

Moses tells us, "The secret things belong to the LORD our God, but the things revealed belong to us and to our sons forever, that we may observe all the words of this law" (Deut. 29:29). God is keeping a secret from the mommies of the world. But they are not the only ones who long for an answer to their question about time.

Why is our growth in Christian character often slow to

come? No matter how you cut it, the sanctification process takes time. And that means that our most troubling vices do not go quickly to the grave. There are seasons in the Christian life when God fast-forwards us in leaps and bounds; on gospel wings we soar above the churning waters of the world, the flesh, and the devil. Yet more frequently we grow through many small, slow steps. All of us know the dark discouragement of trudging through troubled waters. Soaked, muddy, and exhausted, we cry, "How long, O Lord—how long?! I've been a believer for ten, twenty, thirty, forty, fifty years, and still I sin the same old sins. I'm still angry, still fearful, still unloving, still jealous, still proud, still apathetic. Shouldn't I be further along by now? O Lord, how long?"

Our modern culture, with all its bells and whistles of efficient contemporary design, is persuaded by pragmatism. Delayed gratification is so 1900s. We are living in the era of *now*. Want a product? Click it now. Want an answer? Text it now. Want entertainment? Stream it now. The attitude of our culture insists that if it doesn't work for me right now, the way I want, then it doesn't work.

We bring this philosophy about the physical realm into the spiritual realm. The challenge of spiritual growth is compounded by our expectations for a speedy recovery. We realize that a problem with sin exists in our lives; we want it to change; we fight diligently to move beyond ensnaring sin—but change comes slowly. Similar to other areas of life, we assume that spiritual freedom will inevitably be accomplished, fully and finally, now. Our expectations go unmet, and despair sets in.

Slow Movers for a Reason

Why are many of us slow movers in the Christian life? An obvious answer is that our fallen condition has dulled our response to God's truth. But why doesn't God just turn our spiritual dials to high speed, ramping up our rate of progress? Why does it seem that many of our sins will only die the death of a thousand blows?

In God's infinite mind, there are likely a myriad of wise reasons for this. But I believe that one aspect of the Christian life is a critical part of our trouble with diehard sins: we are prone to wander. Do you feel it? Our sovereign, wise, and good God often prescribes slow progress in the Christian life in order to prevent us from trusting in our own power and plan. We have a propensity to trust not in God's power and wisdom but in our own supposed ability to change. Every book that offers "twelve easy steps to an improved you" flies off the shelves.

With the smallest nudge, we buy in to the quick fix—but the quick fix can never make good on its audacious promises. Jeremiah warns us, "Cursed is the man who trusts in mankind and makes flesh his strength, and whose heart turns away from the LORD" (Jer. 17:5). When growth is least quick to appear, we are unable to boast, "I'm doing it! My plan is working! My strength is enough!" When change is slow, we are drawn to beg for God, not to boast in ourselves. We say, "How long, O Lord? Please help me!" It's the sweetest spot in the Christian life. Although God hates sin and has a plan for its ultimate demise, until then He is bending it to accomplish His will. Our prolonged struggle with sin is a tool by which God draws us to Himself.

This was the experience of persecuted Christians in the New Testament. Paul writes, "Indeed, we had the sentence of death within ourselves so that we would not trust in ourselves, but in God who raises the dead; who delivered us from so great a peril of death, and will deliver us, He on whom we have set our hope" (2 Cor. 1:9–10). The slow—sometimes agonizing— death of sin drains our self-trust and drives us to a higher hope,

who is God Himself. Can you be content with this? To enjoy
the reward, to enter joyfully into the fight, we must submit to
God's slow-paced program for change.

Contented Discontent

Much of the Christian life is counterintuitive, and this is
true of our dealings with sin as well. A call to *discontent* over
our remaining sin does not surprise any of us. The true believer
remains the most unsatisfied person in all the world, hating
his sin and longing to see it abolished. As followers of Christ,
we long to see our wicked adversary put to shame, along with
every sinful burden in which he has played a part. A faithful
Christian knows the ability of sin to rob her of God's goodness. She will settle for nothing less than full freedom from sin,
and she will not rest until Christ ushers in the final promise of
His sinless kingdom. This is the good and right discontent that
ought to characterize every faithful believer.

But discontent is not the only secret of fighting wisely
against sin. You may be surprised to read that Christians ought
also to become *content* with sin. Sin is here to stay. God has
providentially ordained that it remain a part of our lives until
a glorious day when He will banish every thorn and thistle left
behind by the fall. No matter how much we dislike the thought
of a prolonged battle with sin, we must become content with
what God has decided about sin's remaining power and presence
in our lives. If not, we will continually falter under a nagging
sense that the Christian life just isn't working for us.

Expectations are dangerous. As easily as proper expectations
foster encouragement, false expectations drive us to despair. To
live rightly before God requires that our expectations fall in
line with His promises. If you expect, in this life, to arrive one
day at a place of super piety, where the thorny pricks of your

sinful nature cease completely, then disappointment will follow you all the days of your life.

God has not promised us an easy, sin-free parade into His Celestial City. There is only one place where thorns and thistles grow no more: in the new world promised by God in the gospel. When we sit down at the wedding feast of the Lamb, this book will not be on the shelves of His extravagant banquet hall. The fact that you are reading it means that you're not there yet. And the fact that you're not there yet means that you must become content with the presence and power of sin in this life.

Does this mean that we ought to give up the fight? After all, isn't that what it means to be content with the presence of sin? May it never be! Becoming content with the reality of our sin and the slow march of spiritual growth is not an excuse to rest on our laurels. Quite the opposite. As we come to terms with the true nature of our fallen condition and agree with God about what to expect in this life, our determination to kill sin will grow. Instead of feeling discouraged by the continual pull of temptations, the relentless exercise of repentance, and the tiresome ups and downs of sanctification, we will run the race with more patience, understanding, wisdom, violence, and hope.

The Priority of Your Position in Christ

Do you enter joyfully into your fight against sin? Or do you lack joy in the struggle? I certainly need more. We won't find this joy by obsessing about how well we're doing as Christians today; we will find it by looking up to Christ, in whom we are fully sanctified before God. This way we will gain a renewed joy and zeal for the ongoing work of sanctification here and now.

The Process of Sanctification

The process of sanctification is a major theme of this book, and rightly so. For by grace we are conformed over time to the image of God's Son. Sanctification may be likened to the gradual upward movement of an escalator, as it carries us ever closer to Christ. The Westminster Shorter Catechism says that sanctification is "the work of God's free grace, whereby we are renewed in the whole man after the image of God, and are enabled more and more to die unto sin, and live unto righteousness."[1] Every faithful Christian longs to grow up into Christ (see Eph. 4:15).

But here comes another unexpected twist: there is a caution against placing too much hope in the process of change. We're under a kind of delusion if we believe that X amount of Bible study plus Y amount of discipline times Z amount of accountability equals the extermination of a particular sin problem. And a desire for a good thing morphs into a bad thing when it is elevated to an ultimate thing.[2] Freedom from the power of our diehard sins is a good desire—until we demand that it happen on our terms and in our time. It is possible to become ensnared by the desire for accelerated spiritual change. Placing ultimate hope in the process will lead to ultimate discouragement when change doesn't come as quickly as we want. For this reason, Scripture calls for our hope to rest on a higher plane: our position in Christ.

The Position of the Sanctified

When addressing our need for spiritual growth, Scripture most frequently describes what theologians call *positional*, *definitive*, or *relational sanctification*. It has much more to do

---

1. Westminster Shorter Catechism, answer 35.
2. Timothy Keller, *Counterfeit Gods: The Empty Promises of Money, Sex, and Power, and the Only Hope That Matters* (New York: Riverhead Books, 2011), xix.

with who we are in Christ than with how quickly we are changing now. The Bible refers to sanctification primarily in terms of God's work to secure us in His favor through the finished work of Christ. In addition to sanctification being like an escalator, Scripture presents it as something like a chair: a place where you and I have been firmly seated, a position given to us by Christ, a relationship through which full righteousness is granted to us.[3]

This means that our assurance is planted firmly in an unwavering hope. Our *likeness* to Christ may ebb and flow across the seasons of life, but our *position* in Christ is set in stone. See the priority of our position in Christ, and its empowering connection to increased spiritual maturity, in Paul's words to the Colossian church.

Our Sanctified *Position* in Christ

Therefore if you have been raised up with Christ, keep seeking the things above, where Christ is, seated at the right hand of God. Set your mind on the things above, not on the things that are on earth. For you have died and your life is hidden with Christ in God. When Christ, who is our life, is revealed, then you also will be revealed with Him in glory. (Col. 3:1–4)

Our Sanctified *Progress* in Christ

Therefore consider the members of your earthly body as dead to immorality, impurity, passion, evil desire, and greed, which amounts to idolatry. (Col. 3:5)

---

3. See David Peterson, *Possessed by God: A New Testament Theology of Sanctification and Holiness* (Downers Grove: IVP, 1995), 27–49.

First we grasp our status in Christ, then we grow into the likeness of Christ. The Christian life stalls out when the order is reversed.[4] Keep this order in mind as you continue reading.

The Promises of Your Position in Christ

Instructing his Scottish congregants to treasure their position in Christ, nineteenth-century pastor Robert Murray M'Cheyne commended to them a simple principle: "For every look at yourself, take ten looks at Christ." He knew the value of prioritizing his heavenly status as a means of fighting sin. M'Cheyne continued, "Let your soul be filled with a heart-ravishing sense of the sweetness and excellency of Christ and all that is in Him. Let the Holy Spirit fill every chamber of your heart; and so there will be no room for folly, or the world, or Satan, or the flesh."[5]

Perhaps you've heard this famous quote but have struggled to discern its application to your life. What does it mean to look at Christ in a meaningful way? What exactly are we looking at? There is not enough ink in the whole world to be able to write the infinitely glorious answers this question deserves. If we could gaze on Christ for millennia on millennia, we would only *begin* to know the extent of His greatness. When we look at Christ, we find that all God's eternal promises receive their "yes" in Him (see 2 Cor. 1:20).

Let's consider three of the gracious promises we have through our union with Christ—promises that, when rightly embraced, can fuel our sin-killing endurance.

4. We may also refer to this order as the indicative/imperative dynamic. First we are grounded in what Christ has indicated about us (our position), and then we are able to obey His imperatives (our progress).

5. Andrew Bonar, *Memoir and Remains of Robert Murray M'Cheyne* (repr., London: Banner of Truth, 1966), 293.

Promised Favor

In Christ we receive the promise of God's loving favor, full and free. We have done nothing to earn His favor. The law of God, written in the pages of Scripture and on the tablets of our hearts, convicts us as sinful, undeserving creatures. Despite our failure to walk in His ways, God has chosen to favor us in His Son. "He [the Father] made Him [the Son] who knew no sin to be sin on our behalf, so that we might become the righteousness of God in Him" (2 Cor. 5:21).

A great exchange has occurred. We who deserved wrath have been made righteous, and He who was righteous has been made to bear the wrath of the everlasting God. By pure grace, through the gift of faith, we are granted a new position before God. We who Jonathan Edwards described as hanging over hell by a spider's web have been plucked from the fire and made sons and daughters of God.[6] Reflecting on the gospel, a friend of mine recently commented that this all seems too good to be true—"It just can't be this easy." I replied, "That's because Christ has taken the burden on Himself and given us His light and easy yoke." What an incredible promise of mercy and grace! Puritan Octavius Winslow exhorts us,

> Oh, how worthy is he of your most exalted conceptions,
>   —of your most implicit confidence,
>   —of your most self-denying service,
>   —of your most fervent love.
>
> When he could give you no more
>   —and the fathomless depths of his love,
>   and the boundless resources of his grace,

---

6. Perry Miller and Thomas H. Johnson, eds., *The Puritans: A Sourcebook of Their Writings* (Mineola, NY: Dover Publications, 2001), 289.

would not be satisfied by giving you less—
he gave you himself.

Robed in your nature,
laden with your curse,
oppressed with your sorrows,
wounded for your transgressions,
and slain for your sins,
he gave his entire self for you. . . .

You cannot in your drafts upon Christ's fullness be too
covetous, nor in your expectations of supply be too
extravagant.

You may fail, as, alas! the most of us do, in making too little
of Christ,
—you cannot fail, in making too much of him.[7]

When we look to Christ once, twice, or ten times, our spiritual eyes behold the promise of God's favor. The psalmist recorded a promise of God's favor to those who would walk in His ways: "For the LORD God is a sun and shield; the LORD gives grace and glory; no good thing does He withhold from those who walk uprightly" (Ps. 84:11). It's a fantastic promise, yes! But are you sure that this promise is for you? Have you walked uprightly so that you may receive the fruit of the promise?

There is no one who does good (see Rom. 3:10–12). How, then, can we rest in His favor? The gospel tells us that Christ fulfilled all the favor-rich promises of God. He walked

7. Tanner G. Turley, *Heart to Heart: Octavius Winslow's Experimental Preaching* (Grand Rapids: Reformation Heritage, 2014), 40–41. The formatting is my own.

uprightly on our behalf, and on the meritorious grounds of His righteousness we live in the favor of God now and forevermore. When sin is slow to die and doubts creep in, remember the promise of God's favor which is yes in Christ (see 2 Cor. 1:20). To look on Christ by faith is to look on His unmerited favor, full and free.

Promised Care

In Christ we receive the promise of God's care for our souls. Whoever wrote the epistle to the Hebrews delighted to dwell on God's incomparable care for the souls of His children. He held fast to his confession of Jesus, "a great high priest who has passed through the heavens" (Heb. 4:14). Jesus, our perfect high priest, stands as Mediator between us and God. Through the redemptive work of Jesus, and by the power of the Holy Spirit, God has had compassion on our souls. He has rested us in His saving arms.

Such incredible care does not happen on a whim. From beginning to end, our salvation has been ordained from eternity past in the mind of God. In dynamic brilliance, the Scriptures reveal how God set on us His covenant love, predestinating our eventual conformity to Christ's image. Down through the ages, His care comes to full bloom. He calls us out of darkness, declares us justified in His sight, and one day will glorify us forever (see Rom. 8:29–30). Oh, how He cares for our souls!

As if His astounding offer of redemption were not wonderful enough, God's promise of soul care extends even into our mundane moments. In Christ we receive not only the promise of redeeming love that secures us, but also the promise that His care will sustain us daily until the end.

The author of Hebrews delights furthermore in this daily offer of transforming and enabling grace. He exalts Jesus, our

High Priest, as the only one who may truly sympathize with the weaknesses of our flesh. The Man of Sorrows entered into our troubles—tempted and tried, as we all are, yet without sin (see Heb. 4:15). From His majestic, rainbow-circled throne flows a heavenly grace, and an earthly grace too. Whether in life or in death, we may confidently draw near to our perfect High Priest. He has grace to save and grace to help in our every time of need (see v. 16).

These two expressions of His gracious care—one that secures us in the heavenlies and the other that sustains us in the earthlies—are intimately connected. No one can tell where one ends and the other begins. The process of spiritual growth, no matter how fast or slow it moves, is carried on under the comprehensive and enduring care of God. To look on Christ is to revel in the promise that He will care for us.

Promised Destination

In Christ we receive the promise of arrival in a perfect, future kingdom. I cringe inwardly whenever I see the popular bumper sticker that reads, "God is my copilot." If I have learned anything from my Christian life, it is that I am unfit to share the wheel with the Lord of glory. Thankfully, none of us is His copilot. Who knows where we might end up? God alone is the pilot of our lives—and He has promised us safe passage to our final destination.

Although many effects of the fall remain in this life, the future heavenly kingdom of Christ will know nothing of this present darkness. Writing about God's promise of a new heaven and new earth, John the Revelator uplifts our souls with the reminder that God will wipe away all our tears, put death to death, and comfort our mourning hearts (see Rev. 21:4). He will cause every last trouble of this life to pass away, making all things forever new. Can you imagine a wondrous place where no one cries, no one suffers, no one develops cancer, no one mourns the loss of a child, no one falls prey to a paralyzing accident, no one grows old and weak, no one is born with a debilitating disease, no one receives abusive blows, no one forsakes another, and no one is forsaken? Such a description only scratches the surface of the future destination we are marching toward in Christ.

In the future city of God, we not only anticipate a world in which our circumstances are free of pain and sorrow but also look forward to our ultimate freedom from sin's power and presence. If you have faced significant loss in this life, you may wonder how exactly God will wipe every tear from your bloodshot eyes. He will do it by leveling a final, crushing blow to sin. He will cast the world, the flesh, and the devil into their rightful place. The old, fallen sin nature will no longer hold us back, trip us up, or blind us from seeing and savoring the all-satisfying grace of our loving Redeemer. The unmistakable presence of God, in His sinless kingdom, will cheer our hearts forevermore.

What is more, this final destination is not a pie-in-the-sky optimism about the future. Through all our trials and temptations, we are being translated (often slowly) to a new home. For good reason, Jesus made future bliss a key point of hope among His disciples. He said to them, and He says to you and me, "If I go and prepare a place for you, I will come again and receive you to Myself, that where I am, there you may be also" (John 14:3). His promise of a heavenly home must become a key weapon in our fight against sin. Along with a myriad of other empowering meditations, we must fight against sin through the regular reminder that this is not the way things will be. "Weeping may last for the night, but a shout of joy comes in the morning" (Ps. 30:5). To look on Christ is to look forward to the promise of His sin-free kingdom. These, and many more biblical promises of our position in Christ, lie at the center of our sanctification.

Fight for Lasting Change over Time

Sanctification has a dual nature. By faith we are fully sanctified in Christ now, yet we also progressively change over time in this life. Through a growing appreciation for our positional sanctification in Christ, you and I will have the motivation and power we need in order to fight for lasting biblical change in our lives.

Focusing on the promises of our triune God is essential, because He is in control of not only our position in Christ but also our growth in grace. Sanctification, positional and progressive, is a Trinitarian work of God from beginning to end. Our continual movement away from sin and toward greater godliness is propelled by God our Father, in the name of Christ our Brother, through the power of His Holy Spirit. By the threefold power of God, we are graciously enabled to put off the old man and put on the new man, according to the full-orbed truth revealed in the Bible.

Lasting biblical change is won over time. In some cases, defeating a particularly resilient sin problem takes a long time. Martin Luther's words are illuminating: "This life, therefore, is not righteousness, but growth in righteousness; not health but healing; not being, but becoming; not rest, but exercise. We are not now what we shall be, but we are on the way; the process is not yet finished, but it has begun; this is not the goal, but it is the road; at present all does not gleam and glitter, but everything is being purified."[8]

8. Martin Luther, "Defense and Explanation of All the Articles," trans. Charles M. Jacobs, in *Luther's Works*, vol. 32, *Career of the Reformer II* (Philadelphia: Muhlenberg, 1958), 42, quoted in William C. Placher and Derek R. Nelson,

By the righteousness of Christ, the apostle Peter directed suffering Christians of his day to see that God's divine power had granted to them everything necessary for godly living in the world. He wrote, "For by these He has granted to us His precious and magnificent promises, so that by them you may become partakers of the divine nature, having escaped the corruption that is in the world by lust" (2 Peter 1:4). The promises of God fulfilled in Christ would be instrumental in helping them to live out their new identity and spiritual position in Christ.

I cannot emphasize this truth enough: your ability to enduringly fight sin is dependent on your daily interaction with the precious and magnificent promises that are yours in Christ. Sadly, frequent reflection on God's promises seems to be a lost art among many of our brothers and sisters. It's easy to neglect this essential aspect of our faith when a sincere desire to become better Christians causes use to lose sight of the bigger picture of life with Christ. Our ultimate reality—being seated with Christ in the heavenlies—lies blurred in our periphery. It follows, then, that an important reorientation for each of us is to bring back into clear view the promises of God. For the wise and faithful follower of Christ, this will be a diligent and continual discipline.

Whether change comes slowly or quickly, God offers joy, purpose, and progress in the fight. Therefore, our ultimate hope is not that we may become sinless in this life, but that we may kill sin by knowing Christ more and more along the way. With real contentment, diehard sinners like you and me can rest in God's promises that are yes in Christ. With our eyes on Christ, we carry a gospel-saturated joy into our fight with sin.

A History of Christian Theology: An Introduction, 2nd ed. (Louisville: Westminster John Knox, 2013), 153.

The next chapter will explore in greater detail our practical plan for fighting diehard sins with joy, wisdom, and purpose.

Reflections for the Fight

1. In what ways have you felt concerned about your own slow progress with changing spiritually?
2. How do you balance contentment with change that comes slowly, on the one side, with a continual discontented desire for change on the other?
3. In your approach to Christian growth, what role does positional sanctification play? How well do you understand your position in Christ?
4. List some ways that you will begin this week to bring the heavenly realities of Christ's finished work back into clear view.
5. Meditate on 2 Peter 1:2–11. Notice the relationship between God's promises in Christ and your ability to practice spiritual disciplines.

Rob's Diehard Sin

Rob is an intense and driven guy. He works in the high-pressure world of high finance, where small details have big consequences. Long days and late nights are common for Rob. When he sets his mind to a task, he works and works until it's done. Rob is a man with a plan. Some people are all about the big picture; Rob captures all the details. Sometimes he can't see the forest for the trees. And he has a plan for where each tree should grow.

But Rob is learning that not everyone at work drops seeds into the nice, orderly rows he has carved out. For every financial portfolio or project, Rob has in his mind a particular blueprint and, with it, an even more particular set of expectations. When his expectations are not met—at work or at home—Rob snaps. Like Zeus, Rob hurls firebolts down on those who thwart his plans. What's worse is that Rob doesn't even know what he's doing until the damage is done. His heart is ruled by his own desires, plans, and expectations. The only way that Rob can change his ways—which he must—is to grapple with the bad roots that are feeding his fiery fruits.

4

The Joy-Filled Fight

The gospel . . . [has] a transforming changing power, into the likeness of Christ. . . . It is a gradual change, not all at once, but from glory to glory, from one degree of grace to another.
RICHARD SIBBES (1577–1635)

Please don't let me die. Please don't let me die. I've frequently found myself pleading with God this way. No, my life has not been full of danger. As far as I know, I'm not at the end of my life—but even if my final breath is just around the corner, I'm not afraid of dying. The reason that I ask God to keep me alive and kicking is because I thoroughly enjoy my life. I have an incredible wife and five kids; I'm thrilled to pastor my church, week in and week out; I have a wonderful crew of loyal friends and family; I relish in extended ministry through counseling and books. Each day I am glad to have a choice from among a handful of meaningful ways to spend my energies. When one happy task is complete, another is waiting its turn at the head of the line.

"Well, that's good for you; it must be nice to live such a charmed life," some may retort. Not so fast. Such joy is a relatively new experience for me. All of us have a level of joy that ebbs and flows. What are at one time enjoyable privileges can sour into grudging responsibilities. True joy does not come from the quality of work we do or from how naturally we take to a given task (though pleasing circumstances do make joy easier). Rather, as Christians, our joy is rooted in Christ and His work in our lives. He fills our good and bad moments with joy. By His grace, Jesus deepens our relationships, gives fruit to our ministries, and transforms our lives in every way—even in our troubles with diehard sin habits.

A Foul-Weather Friend

There is nothing easier to find or to be than a fair-weather friend. When the cotton is high, brotherhood and friendship come naturally. But when the sun scorches the earth and the crops fail, friends pack up and set out.

But Jesus is not a fair-weather friend, and His gospel is not a fair-weather message. Jesus infuses joy and hope into our most difficult moments and our darkest struggles with sin. His loving-kindness makes resisting and mortifying sin a happy work. The days of shrinking back in shame over our failures are replaced with a free and hopeful joy.

For this reason, the apostle James exhorts his readers to endure their many hardships with joy. His New Testament letter was originally addressed to Christians who had been scattered abroad, facing alienation and persecution. Right from the start, James encouraged them to

> consider it all joy, my brethren, when you encounter various trials, knowing that the testing of your faith produces endurance. And let endurance have its perfect result, so that you may be perfect and complete, lacking in nothing. (James 1:2–4)

James, who was most likely our Lord's earthly brother, does not herald his call to joy into only the fair-weather moments of life. Even the sin-touched trials and temptations that we face in this fallen world can be joy-filled challenges. James knows that the loving purposes of Christ bring light and hope into every dark place. Depending on the context of the situation, the word that James uses for *trial* can connote either suffering and hardship that comes from outside us or trials of our own sinful failures. Therefore, you and I are able to follow James's instruction to enter our trials—even the sinful ones—with joy.

Anyone can find happiness on the mountaintop. When you receive your first job offer, when Prince Charming makes your dream of a fairy-tale wedding come true, as a new child bursts miraculously into the world, when the long-awaited promotion is approved, on the first night in your new home, after your hard work pays off in a comfortable retirement. Who doesn't find joy aplenty in these bright seasons? But James reminds us that joy is also available when the clouds of disappointment hang dark and low, when we fail to do right yet again, when the weight of our sin feels too heavy to bear. By faith Jesus has opened the way for us to enabling, sustaining, transforming grace. Are your joy and hope waning as you contend with persistent spiritual trouble? Jesus welcomes you to enter with joy into your daily struggle with sin.

The Right Responses to Sin Habits

Dulce et decorum est pro patria mori is a Latin verse written by the Roman poet Horace. The line is translated "Sweet and noble it is to die for one's country."[1] Horace's enduring verse honors the relatively few brave souls who run with valor into the cross fire. We give thanks for their service and admire their

---

1. Quoted in *The Complete Odes and Satires of Horace*, trans. Sidney Alexander (Princeton: Princeton University Press, 1999), 96.

bravery.[2] I am in awe of true heroes who eagerly leave the training ground for hostile conflict on the battlefield.

Unfortunately, battle-ready excitement in the physical world does not naturally translate into the spiritual world. In the realm of spiritual warfare, we are far less likely to enter with joy into conflict with sin. More often we minimize, shift blame for, make excuses for, justify, or outright ignore our sin struggles. But it doesn't have to be this way. Because our sovereign, wise, and Good Shepherd has joyfully entered our messy, sinful situation, our natural responses to sin are changed.

You Can Face Your Sin Instead of Hiding It

Christ's acceptance of us by sheer grace frees us to deal honestly with the sin habits that plague us. One of the most important Christian freedoms—and one of the most neglected—is the freedom to look our sin in the face. No longer must the ashamed hide their sin away. Jesus frees us to bring our sin into the light of His forgiveness.

Yet this is a daunting challenge for each of us. The law of God, which is written on our hearts, continues its good work of convicting us when we do wrong. When the law uncovers our ungodliness, the old man of flesh instinctively seeks to minimize the seriousness of our problem. When the law sweeps our sin into the air like dust that fills a room, we cough and sputter and head for the door. Rather than facing the ugly truth with the joy of our Advocate, Jesus Christ the Righteous, we hide. As Adam and Eve foolishly hid from God among the trees, we prefer to conceal part or all of our sin.

Do we think that our sin will be less heinous or dangerous if we can drive some of it out of sight or out of mind?

---

2. The Latin is chiseled into the entrance of Arlington National Cemetery, where over 400,000 graves hold the bodies of fallen US soldiers.

Solomon teaches us that "he who conceals his transgressions will not prosper, but he who confesses and forsakes them will find compassion" (Prov. 28:13). In Christ, we are free to confess our sin honestly, knowing that with Him there is grace on grace and a real plan for change.

You Can Own Your Sin Instead of Blaming Others

Entering joyfully into our sin struggles also allows us to take personal responsibility for our failures. As they sought to minimize or hide their sin, Adam and Eve also shifted the blame. When called to account, Adam blamed Eve and Eve blamed the serpent. Pointing fingers didn't help anyone in the garden, and it won't help us now.

Again, God's unconditional election and fatherly care free us to acknowledge our sin personally. Melody, from the introduction, often blamed her sin on other people. Sometimes she was slow to make peace, and other times she was quick to break peace, but all the time she looked for someone else to blame for her ungodly behavior. Are you, like Melody, quick to point the accusing finger? There is good news for you: the gospel can enable you to find joy even in the challenging responsibility of owning up to your ongoing sin habits. Through the cross, Jesus has taken our shame on Himself so that we can embrace our need for change. That means accepting responsibility for ourselves.

You Can Accept Your Sin Instead of Making Excuses

As the gospel gives us grace to acknowledge our sin personally, it also frees us to accept our sin fully and without excuses. We live in a world of misery and trouble and are encircled by evil influences; our spiritual resolve is regularly tested. The world presses in. Pressures of life, losses and crosses, sinful treatment by others, our own body problems, false counsel, the devil, and other influences present us with an endless string of situations to which we must respond.[3] These things are like the sun beating down on us.

Each experience of spiritual "heat" provokes our hearts to release what is already there. If our hearts are directed by godly beliefs and desires, good fruit will emerge. If our hearts are directed by ungodly beliefs and desires, a thorny response will come. In every case, the Bible teaches that we are responsible for our own hearts. God will not allow the temptations, pressures, and trials of life (the heat) to determine our response. Therefore, the responsibility belongs to each of us.

Although it helps us to recognize and understand the influences that we bear in life, these are never to become excuses for our sin—even for our most deep-seated and difficult sin habits. Because Jesus has accepted us by grace, we can joyfully enter into our own sin struggles and accept without excuse the ways that we need to change.

You Can Identify Your Sin as Sin Instead of Minimizing It

Isaiah warns us, "Woe to those who call evil good, and good evil; who substitute darkness for light and light for darkness; who substitute bitter for sweet and sweet for bitter!" (Isa. 5:20). Woe! A more ominous word has never been spoken. Woe is a painful interjection, full of pity and shame. Shame on those who call evil good and good evil. We feel the stinging rebuke.

Yet how often do we continue to defy this truth? We are tempted to hold our sin against the backdrop of other sins and conclude, "It's not so bad. It's not like I've murdered anyone." But comparing ourselves against the standard of other people is unwise (see 2 Cor. 10:12).

3. Timothy S. Lane and Paul David Tripp, *How People Change* (Greensboro, NC: New Growth Press, 2006) 109–32. The metaphor of heat to describe the oppressive forces of the world is developed in detail here.

Our guilt provokes a fleshly desire to make a defense—to locate a reason why the sins we commit are not actually sins. *She had it coming to her. It all worked out in the end. I don't feel that bad about what I did.* We prefer to escape with feigned immunity rather than to face sin with hope.

Jesus's willingness to enter our sinful situation should encourage us to put off our justifications and, by His grace, to seek the real solution: transformation. In His covenant love there is no longer any need to mount a defense before the Judge. Jesus, our Advocate and Defender, has appeased the high court of God.

You Can Acknowledge Your Sin Instead of Denying It

Very few of us would make a blanket statement of denial: "I have no sin." But many of us have ignored and will again ignore outright a habitual sin pattern. In my younger years, for example, I dabbled in video games that violated my conscience. Certain content in the story line or gameplay would arouse feelings of guilt. I repeatedly ignored the spiritual warning light that was blinking on my dash. Over time the small voice of conviction was all but silenced, my conscience lost its strength, and my ugly habit continued until a voice of reproof spoke into my situation.

I had deceived myself—something John warns us about in his first letter. He writes, "If we say that we have no sin, we are deceiving ourselves and the truth is not in us" and "If we say that we have not sinned, we make Him a liar and His word is not in us" (1 John 1:8, 10). Squeezed between these two verses is the antidote to our self-deception: "If we confess our sins, He is faithful and righteous to forgive us our sins and to cleanse us from all unrighteousness" (1 John 1:9). And here is the blazing center of not only our hope in Christ but also our ability to enter our sin battles with joy.

You Can Trust God with Your Sin Instead of Despairing

There is a final caution regarding how we respond to the reality of persistent sin. Under the good conviction of God's law, shame may threaten to pull us into despair. In our moments of weakness, discouragement can so dominate our outlook that hope seems impossible. Despair has a powerful sweeping undercurrent. Routinely, the psalmist groans under the weight of conviction and concern for his sin (see Ps. 38:8). He teeters on the brink of gloom and utter dejection. Yet the knowledge of God's covenant love pulls him back from the precipice.

Have you felt hopeless about your sinful struggles? Have you despaired over what seemed an unsolvable sin problem? How dangerous it is to lose sight of God's grace, mercy, and care! We must fight with every fiber of our being to resist being plunged beneath the surging waves of shame. God is faithful and righteous. He grants forgiveness and cleansing when we turn to Him with our cries for help. As we look to God, who gives joy even in our wrestling with sin, our ability to change grows exponentially.

How to Enter the Fight with Joy

Apart from God's love in Christ, there is no real joy for us in life, let alone in the difficult work of fighting sin. But Jesus brings to us a new lens through which all our times— good and bad—are reinterpreted according to His eternal purposes.

Look to Jesus for Grace

A faithful older Christian once recounted a wonderful illustration of how Christ enables us to joyfully look on our long, slow battle with sin.[4] As a youth, he was consumed by addiction and running wild. God converted him, and his life began to change, but he continued to make his home in the same area of town where he had reveled in wrongdoing. Driven by shame and haunted by the many reminders of his sinful past, he could have fled to a place of anonymity and forgetfulness. Instead, Christ transformed his past, reinterpreting each painful memory as a reminder of God's grace toward him. In the place of shame, this man found a deep and abiding joy. Surely he carried that same joy into his ongoing quest to kill sin, recalling what Jesus did for him.

In the Heidelberg Catechism, sixteenth-century theologian Zacharius Ursinus reminds us of the hopeful, sin-fighting joy we have in Christ. Every believer can say with Ursinus,

> I am not my own, but belong—body and soul, in life and in death—to my faithful Savior, Jesus Christ. He has fully paid for all my sins with his precious blood, and has set me free from the tyranny of the devil. He also watches over me in such a way that not a hair can fall from my head without the will of my Father in heaven; in fact, all things must work together for my salvation. Because I belong to him, Christ, by his Holy Spirit, assures me of eternal life and makes me wholeheartedly willing and ready from now on to live for him.[5]

Through His perspective-transforming kindness, Jesus redeems our sin-born shame and regret and replaces them with a new, living joy.

4. See C. J. Mahaney with Kevin Heath, *The Cross Centered Life* (Sisters, OR: Multnomah, 2002), 13, quoted in Robert D. Jones, *Bad Memories: Getting Past Your Past* (Phillipsburg, NJ: P&R, 2004), 18–19.

5. Heidelberg Catechism, answer 1.

Ask for Wisdom

James the apostle wrote his first-century letter to Christians who were wading through various trials, including their ongoing struggle with sin. James writes, "If any of you lacks wisdom, let him ask of God, who gives to all generously and without reproach, and it will be given to him" (James 1:5). This is a magnificent promise regarding the divine wisdom that we need so desperately. If we will ask God to give us wisdom, He will bless us generously. Any one of us can easily overlook this profound promise of grace.

Many people search everywhere for wisdom except in the God who is there. They look to modern psychologies and self-help gurus, or to television evangelists and talk-show hosts, or to peers, or even within themselves. But Solomon, the wisest man to ever live, writes, "The LORD gives wisdom; from His mouth come knowledge and understanding" (Prov. 2:6). Unless these other voices are informed by the living and active Word of God, their bankruptcy will bear out in the end.

In all the ups and downs you have experienced while dealing with sin, have you asked God for a measure of His abundant wisdom? If not, start asking now. Call on Him in faith to give you everything you need in order to wisely kill your diehard sins. You simply cannot wait another moment. The wisdom that He offers is too good to pass up.

Listen to the way that James describes wisdom two chapters later: "The wisdom from above is first pure, then peaceable, gentle, reasonable, full of mercy and good fruits, unwavering, without hypocrisy" (James 3:17). Our God is the sovereign, wise, and good Ruler of all. His wisdom helps us to understand the important dynamics of our hearts as diehard sins plague us. With reverence and awe, ask the Lord for wisdom daily. He is faithful and will give you what you need.

Become a Student of Sin

When I say this, I do not mean that you or I should sit around devising ways to sin all the more. Nor do I mean for us to become morbidly obsessed with our sin struggles. Instead, we should carefully examine the spiritual troubles that stand in the way of our love for and service to God. It may sound strange, but we need to become students of our own sin.

When I was a teen, studying was of little interest to me. I'm ashamed to admit that I didn't read a single book between sixth grade and the time I graduated from college. Perhaps a little charm and manipulation concealed my neglect of learning. Later in life, I grew to value the spiritual discipline of thinking well, and my study habits rapidly improved.

Many Christians approach the topic of sin in a similar way to how I approached my schooling. At first they see little value in studying sin, so they learn to work around it. But later, when life and sin intersect in more obvious ways, a new wartime mentality is born in their hearts. Are you a diligent student of your own sin struggles? Surely all of us have room to grow in this area.

Because the curse of the law has been removed from us by the life, death, and resurrection of Jesus, we no longer shrink away from making honest observations of sin. Therefore, I want to offer you a helpful tool I have used in my own life— one I have often assigned to others in counseling. Making honest observations of our sin will not only help us know better the ways in which we need to change but will also give us an indication of the progress we are making toward holiness. Throughout our fight against a particular sin habit, we should observe four qualities.

1. *Duration.* When I struggle with _____, how long does the struggle last?

2. *Frequency.* How often do I struggle with _____?
3. *Intensity.* How intense is my struggle with _____?
4. *Triggers.* What else is happening when I struggle most with _____?

Asking these observational questions about your sin will help you to think more carefully about your life. And you shouldn't ask these questions just once. Ask them periodically. As you submit to God's work of change, your answers to these questions may change as your sin struggles improve. Keeping notes in a journal may be of particular help.

The story of Rob, from the start of this chapter, illustrates how these questions work for our good. Rob's short fuse and high expectations produced outbursts of anger. As he grew to hate his angry response to others, he made dedicated efforts to become a joyful student of his sin. Rob's journal shows that in the early stages his anger spells lasted for more than two hours. When he encountered poor performance among his project management team, Rob's anger would begin to simmer. He would dwell on his frustrating circumstances until his disappointment boiled over in rage. It would take another hour for Rob to finally simmer down. But as God's work of sanctification addressed the sinful sources of Rob's anger, his angry hours turned into angry minutes and eventually reduced to irritated moments. He was improving, and he knew it. Rob's growing knowledge of his anger encouraged him all the more to kill his sin.

Rob's journal also showed an improvement in the frequency and intensity of his angry explosions. Once a daily occurrence, his failures became fewer and farther between. His coworkers enjoyed having fewer volatile exchanges with Rob, as he put off anger and put on love. Finally, Rob found much help in observing the circumstances and situations in which he was most likely to give full vent to his anger. Recording these common triggers in his journal, and discussing them with his pastor and accountability partner, gave Rob a certain amount of foresight about occasions in which he could experience heightened temptation to anger.

Prepare for Action

After turning to Christ for enabling grace and committing ourselves to thinking wisely about sin, we must prepare for action so that we may enter joyfully into our conflict with diehard sins.

It is my privilege to serve as a police chaplain in my town. I have always been fascinated by law enforcement, and my appreciation for the dangerous and sacrificial work of officers continually grows. In particular, I have come to value their commitment to preparation. No good officer begins a shift without completing a regimen of readiness. The officers are faithful to ensure that even I am prepared when I accompany them on patrol. I will never forget my first few ride-alongs with our conscientious patrolmen. Once in the cruiser, their first concern was to confirm that I knew the location of the shotgun release button. *If things go south and I wind up holding a shotgun, something has gone very, very wrong*, I thought to myself. But I was grateful for their readiness and foresight. As diehard sinners, we too must be ready for action.

Passivity will not help us to make progress on the spiritual battlefield—action is required. The apostle Peter issues this very command when exhorting readers to be obedient and holy: "Therefore, prepare your minds for action, keep sober in spirit, fix your hope completely on the grace to be brought to you at the revelation of Jesus Christ" (1 Peter 1:13). Literally, Peter instructs us to "gird our loins." The language envisions an athlete or soldier who would pull up the hemline of his flowing tunic and tie it about his waist. Girding the loins provided freedom of movement for running, fighting, or completing a number of other important tasks.

Peter does not mean for us to roll up our pant-legs or dresses, but rather to spiritually prepare for action in the Christian life. Being spiritually ready is a third key to entering with joy into your daily struggle with sin. When you are dressed in readiness for battle with your all-sufficient Captain, fighting sin becomes a joy-filled adventure.

Entering with joy into our daily struggles with sin is the first part of our plan for overcoming diehard sins. Only as we look to Christ to give us freedom and joy to face the dark reality of sin will we be ready to move forward to the second part of our plan: understanding our real needs.

Reflections for the Fight

1. In what ways has Jesus been a foul-weather friend to you? How does He help you in your worst moments?
2. Which of the wrong responses to sin is most evident in your past failure to deal with sin wisely?
3. Think of a diehard sin habit in your life. Begin making observations about your struggle using *Duration, Frequency, Intensity, Triggers*.
4. Meditate on James 1:2–4, dwelling on the joy that Christ brings even to our darkest trials.

PART 2

Understand the True Needs of Your Heart

Frank's Diehard Sin

In the spirit of the skeptical apostle Thomas, Frank's friends aptly nicknamed him "doubting Frank." Frank doubts himself. He doubts his friends. He doubts his past, present, and future. Given the opportunity, Frank could even find a way to doubt his doubts. Worst of all, he doubts God. When he hears a sermon on God's perfect justice, Frank thinks to himself, *it cannot be.* Conversely, when Frank reads of God's perfect love, he disbelieves the riches of His kindness in Christ— *It's not for me.*

You won't be surprised to hear that, as a result of all this doubting, Frank even doubts whether or not his sinful habit of doubting can be changed. He can hear the truth a thousand times, and still he persists in doubting unbelief. His friends at times have wondered quietly among themselves whether Frank is even a Christian to begin with. How can someone who belongs to Jesus still bear so much disbelief? In times of despair, Frank has begun to ask himself the same question.

5

Practicing Sin Detection

*The devil has always his little sins to carry about with
him to go and open back doors for him! And we let one
in and say, "O, it is only a little one." Yes, but how
that little one becomes the ruin of the entire man!*

CHARLES SPURGEON (1834–1892)

Crimes are not solved by victims, witnesses, or bystanders.
They are solved by people who are trained to draw accurate
conclusions from careful thought and observation. Sir Arthur
Conan Doyle's analytical sleuth, Sherlock Holmes, captures
the essence of true understanding. Holmes throws himself
into a crime scene and emerges from a mess of convoluted
clues with evidence that leads to a solution. His keen attention
to detail and skillful data-gathering dispel mystery and make
sense of the case.

Personal spiritual growth calls us to similar investigative
discipline. Thomas Watson wrote, "A man must first recognize
and consider what his sin is, and know the plague of his heart
before he can be duly humbled for it."[1] In order to deal rightly
with the deep reality of sin, we must understand the mess.

---

1. Thomas Watson, *The Doctrine of Repentance* (repr., London: Banner of Truth,
1988), 7.

A healthy self-awareness is critical in the fight against stubborn sin habits. Why do we struggle without achieving the victory we desire? In this chapter we'll do some detective work.

Where Sin Begins

A good friend of mine pastors a young church in Boston. One Sunday morning, the congregation and the elders were set to celebrate the church's sixth anniversary. My friend took to the pulpit and preached an impassioned message about God's abounding grace. As the service closed, stabbing pains drove him straight to the ER. His appendix had ruptured. Has your pastor ever preached so powerfully that he burst an internal organ?

But the ruptured appendix was only half his trouble. To add insult to injury, it took the doctors over seven hours to determine the cause of his pain. Because his medical problem was internal, not external, the hospital staff shuffled around, straining for answers. Three hours after his arrival, a high-tech PET scan was administered but failed to produce a meaningful conclusion. Four more hours passed, and a second, more intuitive scan finally yielded evidence of the rupture. Why was figuring it out so difficult? In spite of incredible advances in medical technology, internal problems are still very hard to see. How much more difficult is assessing the inner workings of our own sinful hearts!

The pervasiveness of sin begins with its immediate location. Sin dwells inside our hearts. Throughout his New Testament writings, Paul consistently exposed the inwardness of his sin. The most significant source of trouble for Paul was not the circumstances of life, the human opponents of his preaching and ministry, or even the spiritual forces of darkness that raged against him. Paul's ultimate foe existed not *out* in the surrounding world but *down* in his own heart. The Christian life is a consuming war against an indwelling adversary: the sinful self.

Even knowing right from wrong and desiring to do good, Paul often failed to cling to the good and hate the evil. To the Christians in Rome, he wrote, "I am not practicing what I would like to do, but I am doing the very thing I hate. . . . I agree with the Law, confessing that the Law is good. So now, no longer am I the one doing it, but sin which dwells in me" (Rom. 7:15–17). By no means does Paul suggest that he is an innocent victim of the fall. Rather, he exposes the troubling reality of inward personal sin. By understanding the spiritual location of sin, his hearers were better equipped to fight wisely against it.

God's clear intention is for us to better understand our hearts according to His perspective. While each of us is two parts—body and soul—the priority in Scripture is on the true inner person, which is described with words like *heart, self, soul, spirit, mind,* and *inner man.* From beginning to end, the war with sin is fought on the veiled battlefield of our fallen hearts.

Where Sin Flows

The heart is the place of our beliefs, motives, desires, priorities, thoughts, and decisions. Is it any wonder why King Solomon wrote, "Watch over your heart with all diligence, for from it flow the springs of life" (Prov. 4:23)? Herein lies our fundamental problem. Sin has hijacked the controls, devilishly influencing every aspect of our lives. There is no part of us that is not touched with the crooked infirmity of evil.

In theological terms, we may refer to this pervasive spiritual malady as the doctrine of total depravity. What ominous terminology! What does it mean for you and me to be "totally depraved"?

First, total depravity does not mean that every person is as corrupt as possible. In His mercy, God holds us back from indulging in every form of sin. Nor does it mean that we have no knowledge of God, for He has ensured that an awareness of Him was left intact. It also does not mean that sinful people like us—even those who are spiritually dead in unbelief—cannot recognize and admire certain virtuous qualities.[2]

What total depravity *does* mean is that every part of our nature is tainted with the corrupting presence and influence of sin. Sin is difficult to kill because every part of us is polluted. My friend did not face only the trial of a damaged organ. During the seven hours in which he went untreated in the ER, a serious infection spread throughout his torso, further complicating his recovery.

If you are reading this book, you have likely experienced the spread of sin in your life. Like cancer crawling through the lymph system, a diehard sin habit has sprouted up in your mind, spread to your tongue, and lurched out through your actions. Sin can advance from a single thought to a life-dominating diehard sin habit.

But giving deserved attention to the difficult doctrine of total depravity need not drive any Christian into despair. Instead, knowing the truth about our pervasive sin nature will help us fight wisely against the very things that so easily entangle us (see Heb. 12:1).

Where Sin Shows

One day I stumbled on one of the creepiest things I have seen in quite some time. An online ad read, "Bye bye, coffins!

2. See Louis Berkhof, *Systematic Theology*, new combined ed. (Grand Rapids: Eerdmans, 1996), 246–47.

These organic burial pods will turn you into a tree when you die." Picture this: when your loved one dies, his or her body can be encased in the root ball of a tree sapling. Once a large burlap sack is secured around the bottom, the pod and tree are planted in the ground. The tree's root system then feeds off the rotting corpse. It's too creepy, right!? I feel queasy just typing it out.

Before I could dismiss burial pods entirely out of hand, I realized there is a sweet sentiment behind burying a loved one in a tree's root ball. It shows the commonsense understanding that all people have: *whatever fruits we see above ground are the direct results of the unseen roots underground.* For this reason, grieving people envision a day when others will see a reminder of lost loved ones flourishing above ground.

Similarly, we know that behaviors come out of who we really are—out of our hearts. Jesus says,

> There is no good tree which produces bad fruit, nor, on the other hand, a bad tree which produces good fruit. For each tree is known by its own fruit. For men do not gather figs from thorns, nor do they pick grapes from a briar bush. The good man out of the good treasure of his heart brings forth what is good; and the evil man out of the evil treasure brings forth what is evil; for his mouth speaks from that which fills his heart. (Luke 6:43–45)

All fruit, whether good or bad, springs up from our hearts— from the real you and the real me. If our hearts are set on truth and godly desires, our lives will surely show it by the righteous ways that we live each day. But if our hearts are set against the truth and ruled by ungodly desires, our lives will surely show it by the evil ways that we live each day. Even seemingly small sins spring out of the heart and reach out of us in a number of tangible ways. If our roots are full of anger and bitterness, then our fruits will reveal it. And if our roots are nourished by a love for God and neighbor, then a righteous harvest will follow.

Gaining a healthy self-awareness—an understanding of our true spiritual needs in the fight against sin—requires us to examine both our roots and their fruits. But one is more foundational and important than the other. The *heart* is the true starting point from which we can understand any particular diehard sin problem.

Picking out the fruits of our lives is a relatively easy task. Fruits are external; they show up in our words and works. Even the unbelieving world, which is blind with sin, can see them for what they are. Jesus taught His disciples,

> Beware of the false prophets, who come to you in sheep's clothing, but inwardly are ravenous wolves. You will know them by their fruits. Grapes are not gathered from thorn bushes nor figs from thistles, are they? So every good tree bears good fruit, but the bad tree bears bad fruit. (Matt. 7:15–17)

What is not so easy to see are the roots that feed our fruits. They are hidden from physical sight. But through the wisdom of God in Scripture and the illuminating work of His Holy Spirit, we can see the unseen. Our Good Shepherd is faithful to show us sheep the heart of the matter, which is a matter of the heart.

Searching for Sin

King David, the great and powerful king of Israel, wrote about his secret sins. "You have placed our iniquities before You, our secret sins in the light of Your presence" (Ps. 90:8).

Our dear psalmist cried out for God to "search me . . . and know my heart" (Ps. 139:23). Why did he need God to search for his sins, unless he felt that they were hidden away out of plain view? And, perhaps most clearly, David wrote in Psalm 19:12–13,

> Who can discern his errors? Acquit me of hidden faults.
> Also keep back Your servant from presumptuous sins;
> Let them not rule over me;
> Then I will be blameless,
> And I shall be acquitted of great transgression.

The term *presumptuous* refers to transgressions that we knowingly commit, even with pride.[3] The Hebrew word literally means overconfidence. David asks God to restrain his willful, adamant sinfulness—those sins that are right before his face and yet he commits them anyway.

That's not all. Another kind of sin weighs on David's mind. If you read with haste, you might skim right over David's concern for the secret sins. For even the incognito sins, he beseeches Yahweh for acquittal. Who can discern his errors?! King David—the giant-slaying, nation-conquering, mighty-men-assembling, take-what-he-wants king of Israel— is afraid of being ruled over. He has met his match. All his valor and might cannot acquit him or keep him back from his innumerable presumptuous, secret sins.[4]

3. John Calvin, *Commentary on the Book of Psalms*, vol. 1, trans. James Anderson (Bellingham, WA: Logos Bible Software, 2010), 330.

4. "We should remember that we are not guilty of one offense only, but are overwhelmed with an immense mass of impurities. The more diligently any one examines himself, the more readily will he acknowledge with David, that if God should discover our secret faults, there would be found in us an abyss of sins so great as to have neither bottom nor shore, as we say; for no man can comprehend in how many ways he is guilty before God" (Calvin, 329).

We must agree with the prophet Jeremiah when he writes,

The heart is more deceitful than all else
And is desperately sick;
Who can understand it?
I, the LORD, search the heart,
I test the mind,
Even to give to each man according to his ways,
According to the results of his deeds. (Jer. 17:9–10)

The grand problem of sin is unsolvable without God's help. He alone can search the heart and know the mind. Since God is the great heart-knower, He has revealed in the Bible His intimate knowledge about our hearts.

Do you regularly cry out to God to kill your secret sins? With His help, you can learn to uncover your hidden faults. Remember that David did not pray for God only to search and know his heart, but also to see if there be any wicked (hurtful) way in him and to lead him in the everlasting way (see Ps. 139:24). I believe that God answered David's prayers, even through the painful gift of Nathan's confrontational rebuke (see 2 Sam. 12:1–15). Therefore, we should take comfort and action from knowing that God has an everlasting way to deal with our sins.

One of the first actions we can take is to submit our lives to God, that our destructive, daily sin habits might become clear before our eyes. We'll start doing this next.

Sin's Three Fronts

We daily face a three-front war against a pervasive enemy within us. As wise soldiers learn the contours of the battlefield before marching out, it helps us to know where the enemy of sin operates. If we don't understand the role of thoughts, words, and actions in our daily quest to kill sin, we forfeit a serious advantage in the fight.

Thoughts

Ask a person to point to the source of his thoughts and he likely will tap his head. But what does the Bible say about the place where our thoughts live and die? The Word of God points to the heart.

In Romans, Paul tells the tragic story of sin. Notice the relationship between darkened hearts and futile thinking: "Although they knew God, they did not honor him as God or give thanks to him, but they became futile in their thinking, and their foolish hearts were darkened" (Rom. 1:21 ESV). The author of Hebrews says that the Word of God judges the thoughts and intentions of the heart (see Heb. 4:12). And Solomon says, "As [a man] thinks within himself, so he is" (Prov. 23:7).[5] Our thoughts originate within our hearts, where sin is present as well.

Dutch theologian Abraham Kuyper referred to sin's corrupting influence over our thinking as the *noetic effects* of sin. It is not that sin has killed our ability to think keenly about life, but instead, without the corrective of God's wisdom, sin distorts our thinking and darkens our outlook on life.[6] Cornelius Van Til imagines a carpenter with his buzz saw sharpened for work. He measures and marks the boards according to the task at hand. However, he doesn't realize that one of his children has sneaked into the shop and changed the setting of the blade. Every cut that he makes is slanted instead of straight. In a similar way, sin has changed the setting of our minds; every

5. Literally "As a man reckons in his soul."
6. See Greg Bahnsen, *Van Til's Apologetic: Readings and Analysis* (Phillipsburg, NJ: P&R, 1998), 154.

thought cuts at a slant, distorted by the faulty setting of sin.[7] Thus, a basic, undeniable necessity of biblical change is the method of "listening for unbiblical thinking and countering with biblical truth."[8]

Frank was riddled with thoughts of doubt and despair. His struggle with a diehard sin habit was inextricably linked to his undisciplined thoughts about God, himself, and the world. He suffered under the pervasive nature of sin within his unrenewed mind. This is why Paul urged the Christians in Corinth to scrutinize the various thoughts that their opponents tempted them to believe (see 2 Cor. 10:5).

In a similar way, we too have skepticism about our own thought lives. In order to effectively fight against sin, our battle plan must include our paying careful attention to what we think: our beliefs, thoughts, affections, intentions, ruminations.

Words

On nearly every page of Scripture, the value of words leaps out at us. The creator God spoke the world into existence. Through words, God Himself has spoken to us. By His words He revealed His thoughts. Perhaps the value of words is seen no more clearly than in the gospel message. The gospel is not a list of commands to follow or a set of instructions for meriting God's favor. Rather, the gospel is an announcement of good news about what Jesus Christ has done for us. It is a declaration of God's promise-keeping purposes in Christ. God has given words a central place in His world. Therefore, we too ought to consciously guard our words.

If left uncontrolled, our sin-sick thoughts will spill out in

---

7. See Cornelius Van Til, *The Defense of the Faith*, 4th ed., ed. K. Scott Oliphint (Phillipsburg, NJ: P&R, 2008), 97.

8. This simple description of the essence of biblical care, counseling, and discipleship was taught to me by Professor Frank Catanzaro. After all I have read and

ungodly communication. Our Lord warned the Pharisees and bystanders that "the mouth speaks out of that which fills the heart" (Matt. 12:34). Have you seen in your own life the pervasive effect of sin on your words? Perhaps this week—or even today—you have said something that showed the dark reality of sin. A sharp word toward your spouse. A curse at an erratic fellow driver. A shout at an erring child.

Kristen, who was diagnosed at the start of chapter 3 with foot-in-mouth syndrome, knew all too well the relationship between a sinful heart and unsavory words. Early in her attempts to understand and tame her unruly tongue, Kristen was tempted to blame her verbal indiscretions on the people or circumstances in her life. "If my boss had been less intense during the meeting, I wouldn't have raised my voice." "Sometimes I just need to vent." "God made me with a blunt way of speaking." As she learned the heart-centered truth about words, Kristen realized that she could no longer blame her insensitive way of speaking on anyone or anything except her own heart. Through the wise care of faithful friends, Kristen saw God taming her tongue by changing her heart.

Gaining freedom from sin's pervasive effect on the words that we use is not easy. James expressed in striking terms the importance of sinful speech. "If anyone does not stumble in what he says, he is a perfect man, able to bridle the whole body as well" (James 3:2). Have you ever known someone who didn't sin with his words? James says that he would be a perfect man!

Jesus did not speak one evil word, but this is a major problem for the rest of us. James expounds on our untamed tongues.

---

learned about the art of discipleship, this simple definition rings true in my heart time and again.

With it we bless our Lord and Father, and with it we curse men, who have been made in the likeness of God; from the same mouth come both blessing and cursing. My brethren, these things ought not to be this way. (James 3:9–10)

The curse of sin has reached up from our hearts and across our lips. But that's not all.

Actions

As words proceed from our troubled hearts, deeds also reveal our fallen nature. When teaching on the heart's central role, Jesus confirmed that "out of the heart come evil thoughts, murders, adulteries, fornications, thefts, false witness, slanders" (Matt. 15:19). He mentions not just evil thoughts and sinful words but also various sinful actions that proceed out of the heart. Murders. Adulteries. Fornications. All very serious transgressions!

Even though you probably aren't facing a murder charge as you read this, the same sinful hearts that are portrayed on prime-time TV are responsible for the daily diehard sins that this book is about. The same heart-level inclinations that produce murderous outrage or lead a person to violate the marriage bed also stand behind the everyday sin habits of housewives and handymen.

Sin Pervades, but Grace Abounds

Is all this talk of sin's spread upward and outward discouraging you? If sin is so widespread in our hearts and lives— even touching our very thoughts, words, and actions—is there any hope? Yes, there is abundant hope for diehard sinners like us! Though our sins have permeated every nook and cranny, God's grace in Christ abounds further still. No matter what we have done, how we have failed, or how far it seems our sin has spread, the God of all comfort knows where we are, assesses our situation, and gives us grace for every need. He had the first word, and He will have the last. Because we know that our Lord reigns over all—including our ongoing struggle against sin—we can face our stubborn habits with joy. In every remembrance of our past failure and in every present temptation, we must look to God for grace.

Puritan pastor John Bunyan is known best for his book *Pilgrim's Progress.* Bunyan's main character, Christian, represents every follower of Christ. Weighed down by the backbreaking burden of sin, Christian must follow the gospel-illuminated path toward a celestial city.

There is little doubt that the author thought of his own sinful trials when writing about his troubled, heaven-bound pilgrim. Raised among the impoverished families of Elstow, England, Bunyan reveled in rebellion. He wrote of his early life, "It was my delight to be taken captive by the devil at his will: being filled with all unrighteousness; that from a child I had but few equals, both for cursing, swearing, lying, and blaspheming the holy name of God."[9]

Around 1652, Bunyan was converted under the faithful influence of his pastor, John Gifford. Eight years later, he was arrested for preaching the gospel without the king's approval. During a twelve-year prison sentence, Bunyan wrote prolifically, producing *Pilgrim's Progress* and his autobiography, *Grace Abounding to the Chief of Sinners.* Bunyan endured his ongoing matches with sin by maintaining a grace-infused life and worldview. In the preface to his biography, he wrote, "Oh, the remembrance of my great sins, of my great temptations, and

---

9. Quoted in Joel R. Beeke and Randall J. Pederson, *Meet the Puritans: With a Guide to Modern Reprints* (Grand Rapids: Reformation Heritage, 2006), 101.

of my great fears of perishing for ever! They bring afresh into my mind the remembrance of my great help, my great support from heaven, and the great grace that God extended to such a wretch as I."[10]

As we continue to explore the nature of diehard sin habits, pray that we will follow with courage and humility in the footsteps of this profound puritan pilgrim.

Reflections for the Fight

1. Do you typically see sin as outside you or inside you?
2. Is there a particular diehard sin that you see affecting your life pervasively? How would you describe it?
3. Which category of sin do you find most apparent and troubling in your daily life: outward (against people) or upward (against God)?
4. In what ways do you need to cultivate a grace-infused outlook on your sin struggles? In Christ, grace abounds to you. How well do you know this?
5. Spend time meditating on the throne of grace that is revealed in Hebrews 4:15–16.

10. John Bunyan, *The Pilgrim's Progress from This World to That Which Is to Come and Grace Abounding to the Chief of Sinners*, ed. John F. Thornton (New York: Vintage Books, 2004), 275.

Mark's Diehard Sin

You'd never know that Mark struggles with a diehard sin. In nearly every way, Mark appears to be the model Christian. He knows the Bible well, his fellow church members frequently ask his advice, and he is scheduled to bring the offertory prayer on most Sundays. His family is in order. His wife is a gem. His children obey in color-coordinated splendor. And in everything Mark does, he prospers. Mark is a model Christian.

But beneath the surface, a diehard sin secretly controls Mark. His stomach is his God. Well, actually, it is more accurate to say that his stomach is a god, ruling his affections from the inside out.

Now, an appreciation of food and drink is common to humanity. In one sense, it is hardwired within us. But for Mark, it's a different and more intense story—a story of addiction, gluttony, and tastes run amok. Every day, Mark is quietly driven along by his love of exquisite meals, savory snacks, and the uplifting buzz of caffeine that he says gets him through his day.

Hearing about Mark's diehard sin might make you uncomfortable because you identify with his respectable addiction. Nevertheless, for Mark and you and me, a simple addiction to food or drink is still exactly that: an addiction.

6

Who Rules Your Heart?

Extol and magnify God's mercy, who has adopted you into his family; who, of slaves, has made you sons.
THOMAS WATSON (1620–1686)

I was enslaved. What seemed like a harmless substance ruled me every day for two decades. Not many would consider my abuse of caffeine to be sinful, but it was. At first light I cracked open a caffeinated beverage, and I kept on cracking them right up to the moment I laid my head to rest at night. I thought nothing of it until I began a course of helpful self-examination. I spent time reviewing key areas of my life, looking for daily addictions that had escaped my attention. My caffeine habit surfaced quickly.

None of my family or friends recognized my habit as a problem, and they certainly did not label my small-time addiction as evil. If anything, caffeine appeared to increase my productivity and happiness. Unlike more well-known addictions, caffeine dependence didn't lead me to neglect my family, fail in ministry, or suffer serious physical maladies. I wasn't spending obscene amounts of money, fraternizing with hardened criminals, or evading the authorities in order to get my fix. I was simply going about my days and trying to serve Christ, love my family, shepherd my church, and be a good neighbor. All the while, I was oblivious to my servitude. Caffeine was the focal point of my day. I felt unable to survive without it.

- I'm feeling tired. Time for a bottle of Mountain Dew. (91 mg)
- My head feels dull. I'll take a headache powder. (32 mg)
- I'd like to stay up late tonight. A large coffee will do. (400 mg)
- Road trip! I'll pick up an energy drink. (80 mg)
- I feel the afternoon slump coming on. How about a chocolate bar? (70 mg)
- Look! My wife bought a 24-pack of Coca-Cola! (816 mg)

When I realized how much caffeine had mastered me, I was concerned about the effect so much caffeine might have on my physical health. But what caffeine meant to my spiritual health concerned me more. To be clear, caffeine is not sinful: there is no biblically derived prohibition of it, and it can be a helpful tool when used wisely. But caffeine became a bad thing when my desire for it ascended the throne of my heart.

By God's grace I am now free from this enslavement. I often wonder, though, to what other yokes of slavery I have given myself. Have you considered this question about your own life? In what ways have you become enslaved to the ruling desires of your heart? "It was for freedom that Christ set us free; therefore keep standing firm and do not be subject again to a yoke of slavery" (Gal. 5:1). Christ has set us free! What better reason could we have than this to take the enslaving power of sin seriously?

When the Bible speaks of sin's enslaving power, it paints a different picture of slavery than the one we might imagine, of a slave being victimized by an oppressive master. Sin is certainly oppressive, but we are not victims. We are willing participants. Spiritual slavery—in all its forms—is a voluntary experience. We are not taken captive by sin against our wills. Indeed, it is our fallen wills that make the defeat of sin elusive. All slavery to sinful desires and ways is caused by our willful participation. Our fallen hearts are prone to slavery. We willingly obey the impulses of our sinful nature and, through daily practice, are immured in a corresponding way of life.

Do you remember Rob, who regularly excoriated his coworkers for not toeing the line? In his worst moments, Rob lived as a slave to his own perfectionistic demands and expectations. However, he was not a victim dragged kicking and screaming into furious explosions of wrath. He was an active agent. Once Rob took ownership of his angry compulsion for control, his rigid ways began to soften. A growing knowledge and understanding of sin's enslaving power infused Rob with strength to fight wisely against his diehard sin habit. If you and I will follow Rob's path of transformation, we too will understand the nature of spiritual slavery.

The Spiritual Slavery Trio

In every instance, slavery to sin involves three factors.

First, there is a change of master as we temporarily defect from the true God in search of a more appealing master. Just as it happened on that fateful day in the garden of Eden, temptations lure us away to seek satisfaction in a counterfeit kingdom.

Second, as our distance from God grows, our blood-bought identity in Christ escapes our attention. We become disordered servants who wander around in a fog of spiritual amnesia about who we really are.

Third, confusion over who we are and to whom we belong leads us to offer a misplaced obedience. Rather than obeying the truth, we give deference to the lies and lusts of our flesh.

Each piece of the spiritual slavery trio is integral to the puzzle of persistent sin habits. What follows is a closer look at each of these three dynamics.

Master: Who Rules Your Heart?

When you war with diehard sins, start by asking yourself, "Who is my master?" Every believer has the Lord as his or her Ruler. Yet in daily life, other rulers vie for control over us. Every morning, you are engaged in a spiritual war to determine who or what will occupy the throne of your heart. There are myriad masters to choose from. Do you hear the siren songs of these counterfeit gods, wooing you to give your heart to them?

The Bible teaches that no one can serve two masters. If you try, the result will be hatred of one or the other (see Matt. 6:24). Therefore, we must choose one. For those who are in Christ, the choice is obvious. No other master can compare with the sovereign, wise, and good God of our redemption! Yet in the hustle of life, the wise choice does not always seem so obvious. The potential for material gain calls out from the marketplace. A sinful craving for approval lures us to fear men the way we should fear God. The false promise of ease and comfort tempts us to escape from the lives He has planned for us. If we are not alert, we sell ourselves into the servitude of sin. Such is the struggle against diehard sins. There is a better Master.

Just as death is no longer master over the Lord Jesus who was raised from the dead, so sin is no longer master over us who were raised along with Jesus (see Rom. 6:8–11). We are to consider ourselves dead to sin and alive to God. Jesus called out to the wayward slaves of sin,

Come to Me, all who are weary and heavy-laden, and I will give you rest. Take My yoke upon you and learn from Me, for I am gentle and humble in heart, and you will find rest for your souls. For My yoke is easy and My burden is light. (Matt. 11:28–30)

Service to Jesus is not laborious and burdensome, but kind and easy to bear. In Christ there is power to escape sin's enslaving control. Yet how often do we find ourselves still languishing under an oppressive yoke of slavery?

Servant: Where Is Your Identity?

Think of the various ways that the Bible describes our identity as believers. God's elect are:

- image-bearers of God (Gen. 1:27)
- known from the womb (Jer. 1:5)
- children of God (John 1:12)
- accepted by Christ to the praise of God (Rom. 15:7)
- united with Christ (1 Cor. 6:17)
- members of Christ's body (1 Cor. 12:27)
- crucified with Christ (Gal. 2:20)
- predestined for sonship (Eph. 1:5)
- hidden with Christ in God (Col. 3:3)
- a chosen, royal, holy people of God (1 Peter 2:9)
- objects of God's love (1 John 3:1–2)

As we consider these striking passages of Scripture, we see clearly the incredible terms that God uses to emphasize our Christian identity. This short list doesn't even begin to scratch the surface of our identity in Christ!

For the Christian, temporarily defecting from Christ to another master requires a serious failure of identity. Christ gloriously purchased us with His blood, yet we live to the contrary. The apostle James compared the experience to a man who looks at his face in a mirror and, walking away, forgets what kind of person he is (see James 1:23–24). To make progress against any diehard sin habit, we must sort out not only what fraudulent master has gained our allegiance but also how our identity has shifted away from the truth.

I recently heard about a fifty-six-year-old German man who lost track of his Volkswagen. We all know the embarrassment of misplacing something so vital—shuffling back and forth as we try not to panic. This poor guy left his car in an industrial parking garage and, when his business there was finished, couldn't recall the exact location. After a lengthy search, his only recourse was to file a theft report with the police. Twenty years later, as demolition workers prepped the garage for implosion, the car was found in an out-of-the-way spot: right where he'd left it. After a painstaking search, the Volkswagen was reunited with its owner—but, unfortunately, two decades of neglect had left the vehicle unsalvageable.[1]

Such an extreme example of parking lot amnesia is hard to believe (and, for the sufferer in the story, even harder to admit). But there are far worse stories of forgetfulness that we all act out every day. In small, repeated steps, we wander farther away from our true identity. Over time, this gradual migration results in the long-term spiritual amnesia of which James spoke. Failure to locate our identity in Christ leaves us foggy-headed about His transforming grace in our lives. We wander about, searching for identity in all the wrong places, on a downward trajectory toward enslavement to a variety of diehard sin habits.

---

1. See Harry Cockburn, "Man Forgets Where He Parks His Car—Then Finds It 20 Years Later," *Independent*, November 16, 2017, https://www.independent .co.uk/news/world/europe/man-forgets-park-car-finds-20-years-later-frankfurt -a8058416.html.

The path up and out of sin always involves a transformation of identity: a return to the rich nature of our union with Christ. Sin habits result from living in ways that are inconsistent with our true spiritual position in Christ. Paul was grievously concerned when he confronted the Galatian believers about this identity failure in their lives: "When you did not know God, you were slaves to those which by nature are no gods. But now that you have come to know God, or rather to be known by God, how is it that you turn back again to the weak and worthless elemental things, to which you desire to be enslaved all over again?" (Gal. 4:8–9). In Paul's mind, the central problem was a failure of identity—the Galatians were living as slaves of sin instead of sons of God. Have you lost sight of the sonship provided to you in the gospel? There is good news: your identity is not unsalvageable. It is preserved by Christ, who never loses sight of you.

Obedience: Who Will You Obey?

Sin is difficult to kill because we are easily enslaved. Because of our original sin nature, slavery to sin comes naturally to us. We are bent by sin to obey its lusts. You have probably heard of an "addictive personality," meaning that a person is particularly bent toward some ruling habit of addiction. In reality, every one of us has an addictive personality. We each will obey someone. We will either obey Christ or obey another master. Either way, there will be obedience.

Scripture depicts the process of spiritual slavery. In James 1, temptation is personified as a luring predator, with a striking feature: the source of this predator is our own desires. "Each one is tempted when he is carried away and enticed by his own lust" (v. 14). Then the lust is conceived in the heart and sin is born. Like an evil child, sin grows up with murderous intentions. "Then when lust has conceived, it gives birth to sin; and when sin is accomplished, it brings forth death" (v. 15).

The process of spiritual slavery begins with temptation, which leads to the practice of a sin habit, which ends in soulish captivity and a perpetual compliance. There is no slavery without obedience to sinful impulses. The battle against diehard sins is very much a question of whom we will obey.

The world, the flesh, and the devil all conspire together to gain leverage in the spiritual war by playing on our inherent desires. These difficult realities are what make slavery to sin so unusual and challenging. Recognizing the relationship between this spiritual slavery trio (master, slave, and obedience) may help us to regain our grip on the truth and put up a wise fight for faith in the midst of a diehard sin habit.

Gospel Emancipation

Near the close of the US Civil War, President Abraham Lincoln issued an executive order: Proclamation 95—the Emancipation Proclamation. Exercising his wartime power, Lincoln's announcement signaled a fundamental change in the status of more than three million slaves and secured victory over the southern Confederacy. African slave trading, which had dominated the landscape for nearly three hundred years, was legally abolished.

From Slavery to Sonship

Slavery is second nature to fallen people—even Christians. We defect from the true Master in order to follow a counterfeit king. We lose sight of our blood-bought identity. We give ourselves as obedient slaves of sin. But there is a transformation that makes an eternal difference: adoption. In the minds of Paul and other New Testament writers, the fundamental transition that opened the door to endurance, hope, joy, and lasting change was sonship.

In Christ, we are not merely converted to a new way of life or a higher way of thinking. We receive a true Master, a new identity, a revitalized obedience. In His gospel emancipation, God grants His elect an entirely new spirit.

> You have not received a spirit of slavery leading to fear again, but you have received a spirit of adoption as sons by which we cry out, "Abba! Father!" The Spirit Himself testifies with our spirit that we are children of God, and if children, heirs also, heirs of God and fellow heirs with Christ, if indeed we suffer with Him so that we may also be glorified with Him. (Rom. 8:15–17)

This Spirit of adoption detailed in Romans 8 offers the supernatural power that is necessary for us to mortify sin, change our ways, and please the great Redeemer who gave Himself for His brethren.[2]

Total Freedom

The meticulous tally records kept by taxpaying slave traders total the number of Africans who crossed the Atlantic in bonds at 12.5 million. But settlers of the New World also enslaved upward of 5 million Native Americans.[3] This smaller in scale, yet equally deplorable, tragedy operated in the shadows of the more recognizable African chattel slavery. The "other slavery," as it was known, persisted with tremendous

2. See David B. Garner, *Sons in the Son: The Riches and Reach of Adoption in Christ* (Phillipsburg, NJ: P&R, 2016), 115–29.

3. See Andrés Reséndez, *The Other Slavery: The Uncovered Story of Indian Enslavement in America* (Boston: Houghton Mifflin Harcourt, 2016) 5.

resiliency because of confusion over whether Proclamation 95 applied to the Native Americans who waited in chains.[4] Not until years after musket fire ceased at Gettysburg did Native Americans know the freedom that was declared to them in Lincoln's executive order.

Similarly, we need the transforming power of the gospel to seep into the lesser slaveries that we face. The gospel is the monumental declaration of freedom by which we learn to obey Christ and disobey sin. Carrying divine authority and power, the good news of Jesus delivers transforming grace to those who may escape from the clutches of sin—not only from the flagrant forms of spiritual slavery like alcoholism, but from the less obvious forms as well.

Many Christians have little trouble embracing the gospel as good news for the most popularized sins and slaveries. "Christ is enough!" is the news they herald. But when faced with the "other slavery"—the lingering, ordinary, acceptable struggles of the soul—those same Christians display serious misgivings about the gospel's power to seep into the crevices where diehard sin troubles live. Is the gospel meant for such as these? The daily anxieties of life, the flaws and faults of ordinary sinners, the trials and troubles of average men and women? Regarding gospel sufficiency, Scripture does not differentiate between complex slavery and simple servitude. In the Bible, sin is slavery and the gospel is enough to free all.

Mastered by the Gospel

In the broadest sense, the gospel includes everything God has graciously done, is doing, and has promised to do to redeem His fallen creation. Viewed more narrowly, the gospel is the good news of Jesus's redemptive rescue mission, by which He

---

4. See Reséndez, 295–314.

lived a perfect life, died an atoning death, and triumphantly rose again for sinners like us. Considering both these broad and narrow views, the gospel intersects all of life. The gospel is the greatest reality in all the world, and it must become the greatest reality in the small personal worlds that we live in every day. Every heart that will be freed from sin is a heart that must first become overwhelmed by the life-transforming message of the cross. And our sense of awe over Christ and His good news must never fade from view.

The truth is that no one "gets" the gospel. None of us can corner it. We will never master the good news as though we could exhaust its power and move on to something better. The gospel must master us, as we continually explore its endless caverns of redeeming grace and truth. We should be careful, then, to avoid a trap that has ensnared many unsuspecting Christians. It is a serious error to believe that the Christian life must be undergirded by a more fanciful principle than the old-time message of the cross, such as man-made self-help principles or the "secret tricks" said to be hidden in modern psychologies—a couple of examples that are ever on the surface of my mind, as a biblical counselor. We must keep the main thing the main thing, and the main thing is the gospel. Are you being mastered daily by the good news of Jesus?

Jesus is not only a freedom fighter who breaks the chains of spiritual slavery; He is a Shepherd who teaches us how to live as citizens of His kingdom. Thus, our continued freedom depends on our hearing daily from Christ the proclamation of that freedom, secured through His cross.

If you are a son, not a slave, and belong to God's growing family, there is hope for you in the fight against sin and temptation. As those who are rescued from the trading block of sin, our entire spiritual status has changed. We are no longer bound as slaves to sin but are sons and daughters of God, giving faithful allegiance and loving obedience to the Lover of our souls. By grace alone, He secured the adoption of His covenant people. Our bonds of enslavement are progressively broken through a growing awareness of and participation in our adoption through Christ.

When each of my children was conceived, he or she was immediately my son or daughter. Their relationship to me was already secure. But, as time passed, each of my children drew closer to me and I to them. It was as though they became even more my sons and daughters, and I became even more their dad.

Through Christ, God is our Father—our relationship to Him is secured forever. At the same time, we are growing up into Christ until one day we will shall finally be like Him, for we will see Him just as He is (see 1 John 3:2). In the meantime, we persist under a propensity for spiritual slavery. But in communion with Christ we are growing and changing through the grace that He gives each day. Through the effectual work of His Spirit our slavery to sin is falling away, and in its place a wonderful, increasing sense of sonship is taking root.

Reflections for the Fight

1. In what ways have your heart and life bowed beneath a yoke of slavery to sin?
2. What sin habits do you struggle to recognize as slavery to a false master?
3. How would you describe your identity in Christ? Are you well acquainted with who Scripture says you have become through the gospel?
4. Spend time prayerfully meditating on Romans 8:15–17. Consider carefully the benefits of your spiritual adoption as a son or daughter of God.

Ken's Diehard Sin

To say he is shy would be a drastic understatement. Not only is Ken's personality shy, introverted, and reserved, but within his introversion Ken suffers from a chronic social anxiety—what the Bible calls "fear of man." In school Ken dreaded class presentations, and now he despises any public scenario in which he must personally interact with other people. Through his own willpower and intellect Ken gets by, but not without a gnawing, anxious feeling.

Although he could keep simply pushing through his anxiety in his own willpower, Ken wants this problem to change. He believes what the Bible says about the sinful fears, anxieties, and worries that so easily entangle us (see Heb. 12:1). He is willing to work diligently to obey what God says about his sinful fear. To run the race set before him, he must begin by addressing the heart of his anxious problem: the problem in his anxious heart. But he's not sure even where to begin—the problem seems beyond his ability to understand or control.

7

The Power of Beliefs and Desires

He, the God of love, so sets himself forth in characters
of endearment, that nought but faith, and nought
but understanding, are wanting, on your part, to
call forth the love of your hearts back again.

THOMAS CHALMERS (1780–1847)

In 1826, famed student of food and culture Jean Anthelme Brillat-Savarin coined the figurative phrase *you are what you eat*.[1] Brillat-Savarin believed that a person's stomach significantly impacted everything else about him. A similar sentiment is seen in our biblical anthropology. A person's heart impacts everything about her. This is true not only in the big moments of life; it's true in the small, mundane moments too.

Once we have entered joyfully into the fight against sin, we must apply God's wisdom to understanding the dynamics of diehard sins in our hearts. We saw in chapter 5 that we are called to be investigators of our sin. Yet we would rather apply our detective skills to other areas. With keen insight we pick apart the story line of a captivating mystery book, scrutinize the intra-office politics, suss out the most rewarding degree

---

1. See Jean Anthelme Brillat-Savarin, *The Physiology of Taste*, trans. M. F. K. Fisher (repr., New York: Alfred A. Knopf, 2009), 15.

track. When a sin problem takes center stage, we throw up our hands and devise a thousand excuses. Our desire to solve the spiritual crime wanes.

Our anxious friend Ken needed to understand why his anxiety was so powerful. He was willing to work diligently to obey what God said about his sinful fear, but he was not sure where to begin; the problem seemed beyond his ability to understand or control. What Ken lacked was a healthy awareness of himself—an understanding of his true spiritual needs as an anxious person.

Being self-aware involves knowing your own heart and life. Like an investigator, you must be willing and able to observe your beliefs and desires and the spiritual fruit that flows from them. How capable are you as an investigator of yourself? Do you take time to prayerfully consider your own motives and values? Throughout the rest of this chapter, I will help you to grow in this important Christian discipline. But first a warning.

Beware the Trap of Introspection

Not all introspection is healthy. When self-examination intensifies, we can fall into a morbid introspection. Our eyes become transfixed on ourselves, and our goals for change become self-centered. Rather than setting our eyes on Christ and trusting Him to change us, we turn inward and become self-preoccupied. When this happens, our objective shifts from pleasing God to fixing ourselves. Urgent pressures to become better Christians or to reform our faults oppressively consume our minds. Self-delusion and self-absorption settle in. Morbid introspection keeps us from loving God and loving people, because we become the reference point for ourselves. Everything begins to revolve around us.

May it never be! There is a better way. We can be self-aware without being self-absorbed. It has everything to do with where we place our hope. Becoming a more considerate person (Kristen), trusting God more consistently (Frank), and leaving behind a gossiping lifestyle (Eliza) are all good desires to have. But, if we place our hope in them, the good desires can turn bad quickly. The alternative is to place our ultimate hope in God's unconditional election and covenant faithfulness, knowing that He is for us no matter how quickly we change.

Under the comforting assurance of God's sovereign grace and love, we are able to examine ourselves without morbidity. The author of Hebrews implores us to fix our eyes on Jesus, "the author and perfecter of faith, who for the joy set before Him endured the cross, despising the shame, and has sat down at the right hand of the throne of God" (Heb. 12:2). If we consider carefully what Jesus has done for us through His cross, the radiant glory of His grace will protect us from the slavery of self-focus. So when you find yourself obsessed with your diehard sins, redirect your focus back onto Christ and the good work He has graciously begun in you.

Between our choice to enter joyfully into a battle against diehard sin and our work to bring Christ and His provisions to bear on it, there is in the middle a need to understand. What exactly do we need to understand before we can rightly apply God's resources for change to our own lives? We must understand the dynamic workings of our hearts: the *desires* and *beliefs* that are the most powerful and influential aspects of our nature. Your endless thoughts, words, and actions flow from a set of beliefs, and every decision you make is rooted in the current desire of your heart. Therefore, the Bible urges us to care deeply about beliefs and wants.

Examine Your Beliefs

Consider Ken. Throughout his life, anxiety has held Ken back from the joy of confidently serving God and people. Fear and worry are his constant companions, and he doesn't know why. At times, Ken wonders if the pressures of work and family are to blame. At other times, bad memories of his traumatic past captivate him as he searches for the root cause. Unable to pinpoint the cause of his anxiety, Ken feels stuck and sometimes hopeless. Despite his investigations, Ken has neglected the source of his anxiety: his beliefs.

In your past attempts to understand your own sin habits, have you overlooked the powerful influence of your beliefs? It's a common oversight. We naturally assume that the problems we face are the result of outside forces pressing in on us. Our natural inclination to look around us, not within us, is reinforced by much modern discipleship. We assume that our hearts are innocent, and we blame outside forces such as people, circumstances, and stressors for perpetuating our sinful habits.

From childhood, many people have embraced a life and worldview that correspond with this assumption. Consider the lyrics to a popular Sunday school song,

> O be careful little eyes what you see
> O be careful little eyes what you see
> There's a Father up above
> And He's looking down in love
> So, be careful little eyes what you see
>
> O be careful little ears what you hear
> O be careful little ears what you hear
> There's a Father up above
> And He's looking down in love
> So, be careful little ears what you hear

O be careful little hands what you do
O be careful little hands what you do
There's a Father up above
And He's looking down in love
So, be careful little hands what you do

O be careful little feet where you go
O be careful little feet where you go
There's a Father up above
And He's looking down in love
So, be careful little feet where you go

O be careful little mouth what you say
O be careful little mouth what you say
There's a Father up above
And He's looking down in love
So, be careful little mouth what you say

What do you notice about each stanza of this cheerful tune? Is something missing? Certainly we should guard our eyes, ears, hands, feet, and mouths, and a loving Father does indeed look down on us all the time.[2] But this song inadvertently neglects our inner lives. We station guards against the corrupt external world while assuming that all is well in our souls.

In rich and insightful ways, our Father sings an additional stanza: "Be careful little hearts what you believe."

Why Watch What You Believe?

I apologize if that song is now stuck in your head, but the truth in that added lyric needs no apology. *Be careful little heart*

---

2. The Latin phrase for this is *Coram Deo*, which is translated "before God's face."

what you believe. Aligning our beliefs with Scripture is imperative to our spiritual maturity.

Your Beliefs Shape Your View of *Everything*

Every person has a worldview—a set of beliefs that he lives by—and his worldview functions like a lens. He gazes through the lens and surveys the vast universe. We each think, speak, and act according to a worldview.

But apart from the worldview of Christian truth, very little can be known or consistently understood in God's world. Thus, our battle against diehard sins is a battle of worldviews. The worldview of Scripture is at odds with the world, the flesh, and the devil. The need for right beliefs is inescapable. Even in the mundane, street-level issues of life, what we believe matters a great deal.

There's more to the story of Ken, our anxiety-ridden brother. After prayerfully exploring the beliefs behind his fear, Ken identified a stumbling block that prevented him from being around other people. All the pastors and mentors who he knew were articulate, well-spoken, extroverted people. Ken so highly valued his articulate heroes that his worldview held little room for shy, inarticulate people like him. He believed that his inability to make natural conversation with others would lead to embarrassment and ridicule. These false beliefs led Ken to retreat from public or personal settings altogether. He had bought into a lie and desperately needed to bring his beliefs back in line with God's truth.

Your Beliefs Will Lead You Closer to God . . . or Farther Away

Right beliefs not only frame a right view of God but also propel us toward greater love for Him. If I believe rightly that God is glorious and all-satisfying, then my heart will be further drawn to magnify Him. But if I believe wrongly that God is limited in power or is unloving, then I will turn away from Him. In the end, my low estimation of Him will be refuted to my shame. Puritan Walter Marshall says, "You cannot love God if you are under the continual, secret suspicion that he is really your enemy! . . . You simply cannot love God unless you know and understand how much he loves you. . . . In the gospel, you can come to know that God truly loves you through Christ."[3] If we are to relate rightly to God, we must first believe rightly about God. Thomas Chalmers writes, "Let us try every legitimate method of finding access to your hearts for the love of him who is greater than the world."[4]

The same is true concerning our fellow image-bearers. Marshall continues, "When you have this assurance, you can even love your enemies, because you know that you are reconciled to God. You know that God's love will make people's hatred of you work together for your good."[5] Neighbor-love demands that we believe what God says about us and others.

Take Kristen, for example. Why does Kristen regularly offend others with her words? Her lack of self-control may be rooted in her failure to understand the people God has placed in her life. Perhaps she has failed to appreciate what God says about the harsh words that stir up anger (see Prov. 15:1). Or maybe she does not believe that a gentle and quiet spirit is precious in the sight of God (see 1 Peter 3:4).

One thing is certain: our beliefs are powerful determiners of how we will relate to other people, as well as to God. Guarding our beliefs should be a high priority.

3. Walter Marshall, *The Gospel Mystery of Sanctification: Growing in Holiness by Living in Union with Christ*, ed. Bruce H. McRae (Eugene, OR: Wipf and Stock, 2005), 31–32.

4. Thomas Chalmers, "The Expulsive Power of a New Affection," in *The Works of Thomas Chalmers, D. D.* (Philadelphia, 1833), 385.

5. Marshall, *Gospel Mystery*, 32.

Your Beliefs Motivate Your Actions

I will never forget a simple equation that someone once taught me:

stated belief – actual practice = actual belief

In other words, we live out what we believe. If a man believes he has a God-given responsibility to care for his family, he will act on that belief by working for, protecting, and loving them (see 1 Tim. 5:8). If a woman believes that God is pleased by her efforts to look after orphans and widows and to keep herself unstained from the world, then she will cheerfully take action to that end (see James 1:27). If a Christian student believes that faith comes by hearing and hearing by the Word of Christ, he will be moved to proclaim the gospel among his friends and classmates (see Rom. 10:17).

Questions to Ask about Your Beliefs

We must cultivate a healthy self-awareness of our beliefs both proactively and reactively.

Proactive awareness comes through practicing daily spiritual disciplines.[6] Prayer, Bible reading, and ministry with other Christians are invaluable practices for every believer. As you remain faithful, the Father works to conform you to the image of Jesus the Son, by the power of His Holy Spirit. According to Jesus's prayer, God sanctifies you in the truth—and this includes the sanctification of what you believe. He plants, waters, and grows His truth in our hearts.

We each have a responsibility to cooperate with Him as He

---

6. To learn more about spiritual disciplines, see Donald S. Whitney, *Spiritual Disciplines for the Christian Life*, rev. ed. (Colorado Springs: NavPress, 2014).

graciously brings us to maturity. It is essential, then, to invest your own time and energy in practices that promote deep roots of belief in your heart. As you continue to pursue the truth, you will become more and more in tune with what you believe and why you believe it.

The other way to maintain a healthy self-awareness of your beliefs is *reactively*. The Christian life is full of mountains and valleys. On the mountains, we feel freedom from enslaving sins. In the valleys, we experience the sting of our failings more acutely. In these difficult and concerning seasons of sin, we must react quickly against our fallen ways. We are often able to learn best during the times when we're at our worst. God can turn your sinful failings into opportunities for growth and change. You can begin to glean from them a deeper understanding of your own heart and can be the better for it.

Frank couldn't shake the doubts that were swirling in his soul. Encouraging pep talks, sound arguments, and loving assurances provided him little relief. Frank was like the surf of the sea, driven and tossed by the wind (see James 1:6–8). In his worst moments of doubt and disbelief, he could sink no lower. Frank wasn't committing gross outward sins. His deadly sins hid in his heart, rooted in the soil of false belief. In order to uproot his doubt with repentance, Frank had to ask questions about his own convictions.

Every diehard sinner ought to harness the skill of interviewing himself. Repentance and change depend on our careful questioning of the beliefs we hold. Here are six such questions that we should ask as we seek to kill the remaining sin habits in our lives:

1. What strong beliefs were at work in my heart?
2. What does this sinful habit reveal about my beliefs?

3. What do my thoughts, words, and actions reveal about my actual beliefs?
4. From where did these beliefs originate? Why do I believe that?
5. Are these beliefs consistent with God's will for me in Scripture? Do I have scriptural warrant to continue in this belief?
6. What sinful beliefs need to be uprooted and replaced with godly ones?

These questions lead us to an understanding of our true spiritual needs.

Examine Your Wants

Just when you thought that the Sunday school song had left your head, we add one more verse: *Be careful little heart what you want.*

At every moment, every person has a heart full of desires. We could even go so far as to say that there is never a time when anyone does what his heart doesn't desire: "The heart wants what it wants, or else it does not care."[7] The heart of man always pursues what it desires most.

This reality can lead to great good or great evil. A heart controlled by a desire to glorify God will produce fruit to the glory of God. On the other hand, a heart controlled by an ungodly desire will produce fruit that is grievous to God. When diehard sins grow, we cannot overcome them without earnest attention to the desires of our hearts.

---

7. Dickinson to Mrs. Samuel Bowles, summer 1862, in *Emily Dickinson Letters,* ed. Emily Fragos (New York: Alfred A. Knopf, 2011), 139.

Sometimes We Want What God Forbids

It should go without saying that a desire to commit murder or to rob a bank or to do some other evil act is always a sinful desire. God has forbidden these desires and actions. But our daily diehard sins are often not the notorious, high profile prohibitions that most people think of as serious sin. We are all capable of wanting forbidden fruit. Such desires accomplished our original fall under sin's curse in the garden.

Sometimes We Want a Good Thing in a Bad Way

A desire for something good—something that God has not forbidden—can quickly grow into a consuming, ruling desire. This kind of desire stands behind most of our ungodly thoughts, words, and actions. Consider the example of Mark. Mark appeared to be a model Christian in every area of life except the dessert table, where his desire for food ruled his heart. Food is a good gift from God; it not only sustains us but also brightens dark days, brings friends and family together, and accompanies special occasions. But when someone's appreciation for a good thing like food becomes a ruling desire, the good gift is spoiled. Rather than bringing joy and delight, it enslaves and controls. Such consuming desires are behind every diehard sin.

We Make Idols

As you evaluate the role of desire—whether for good or evil—in your life, a picture may be worth a thousand words. Imagine that your heart is a staircase.[8] At the base of the stairs is a godly desire for a good thing. At the top of the staircase is

8. This metaphor of the staircase and the throne comes from lectures by Robert D. Jones, which were subsequently updated and published in his book *Pursuing Peace: A Christian Guide to Handling Our Conflicts* (Wheaton, IL: Crossway, 2012), see esp. 65–73.

a throne, and sitting on the throne is our Lord Jesus. By God's grace, Jesus rules our lives from His throne in our hearts. As we keep our eyes fixed on Him, the all-satisfying Lord of life, our desires remain in their proper place at the bottom of the staircase, in submission to Jesus's supremacy.

But not all is well. The sin that remains within us poses many dangers. Although the Captain of our faith reigns and rules, the good desire at the base of your staircase begins to grow and ascend toward the throne of your heart. What you want grows into something that you feel you "need." Before long, this illegitimate need matures into a demand. You will and you must fulfill your desire! And with that, your heart has been hijacked by a consuming lust, which the Bible calls idolatry.

Our Desires Can Drag Us Away

Let's think about our friend Rob—the zealous and hard-working employee described before chapter 4. Rob completes tasks on time and with excellence. He desires high marks on his quarterly review, and he wants his projects to proceed smoothly. Rob desires a good thing. God has certainly not forbidden Rob from planning his work and working his plans. Quite the contrary: our orderly God is pleased when we order our lives (see 1 Cor. 14:40). Yet, as a sinner, Rob can let his desire for orderliness at work become one of his deepest "needs." His rogue desire leads him to place unloving demands on his team members. Eventually, if this desire is left unchecked, Rob will bow before the altar of workplace excellence. His intense, impatient treatment of others at work and at home is not caused by outside forces, such as workplace pressures or incompetent coworkers. His diehard sin habit flows out of a heart that is under siege from idolatrous desires.

The apostle James teaches this very truth clearly.

God cannot be tempted by evil, and He Himself does not tempt anyone. But each one is tempted when he is carried away and enticed by his own lust. Then when lust has conceived, it gives birth to sin; and when sin is accomplished, it brings forth death. Do not be deceived, my beloved brethren. Every good thing given and every perfect gift is from above, coming down from the Father of lights. (James 1:13–17)

God is the Giver of all good gifts, and sometimes those good gifts are sinfully abused. But God is by no means at fault for these failures. He is not a tempter. Instead, James places the onus on the lusts (ruling desires) that rule our hearts. Temptation begins with a small desire. The desire grows into lust. Our hearts are smitten, and sin is born. With time, our sin grows up and kills us.

What is James's warning to us? Be careful little hearts what you want!

Questions to Ask about Your Wants

The idolatry of ruling desires always leads us to sin. In fact, Scripture tells us that all sin is *grounded* in heart idolatry. Paul writes, "Consider the members of your earthly body as dead to immorality, impurity, passion, evil desire, and greed, which amounts to idolatry" (Col. 3:5). Therefore, a faithful investigation of our hearts aims to uncover the rogue wants and desires that fuel our persistent sin problems. How can we know if a godly desire has soured into an idolatrous lust? Fit it in the blanks of the following statements and see if any ring true.

- I am willing to sin in order to have _____.
- I am willing to sin if I don't have _____.
- If I don't have _____, life is not worth living.

- If I can't accomplish _____, I just can't go on.
- If _____ doesn't happen, I don't think I'll ever be happy again.[9]

As elementary as these statements seem, when they are carefully answered, they reveal a great deal about your own heart and the diehard sins that plague you. Follow them up with these three questions.

1. What do I want, and why is this so important to me?
2. Am I desiring something that God has forbidden?
3. Has any good desire soured into an illegitimate need, demand, or idol in my heart?

God's Word Makes the Difference

The psalmist treasured God's Word in his heart so that he would not sin against God (see Ps. 119:11). It wasn't the simple practice of *reading* the Scriptures that made a difference in his life, but rather *treasuring* the Scriptures. What does that mean? When we treasure God's Word in our hearts, our beliefs and desires are thoroughly informed by the truth and lead us in godly ways.

In the New Testament, the apostle Paul urged his spiritual son to pay close attention to his life and his teaching. He taught Timothy to care about not only the ways that he lived but also the inner workings of his heart. Doing so, Paul promised, would eternally benefit Timothy and his hearers (see 1 Tim. 4:11–16). In another passage, Paul encouraged Timothy to continue in the Scriptural sufficiency he had encountered since

9. These questions are commonly used and taught by biblical counselors as helpful questions for self-examination.

childhood from other faithful Christians who clung to God's sacred writings (see 2 Tim. 3:15). Timothy was committed to a lifelong process of growing in wisdom by diligently aligning his heart with God's revealed wisdom.

Down through church history, faithful Christians have striven toward sound theology. The great eras of Christian history are marked by careful attention to doctrine through the writing and reading of catechisms, detailed statements of faith, countless books, and other resources. Likewise, the darkest days of history have accompanied a general apathy for biblical truth. Godly beliefs and affections are of immeasurable value to the progress of sanctification and to our ability to please God. In the part 3, we take a necessary step from understanding our spiritual needs to bringing Christ and His resources to bear on our lives.

Reflections for the Fight

1. As you think about your remaining sin habits, are you prone to obsessing about your struggles? What will you do to gain a healthy self-awareness instead?
2. How do you see ungodly desires and rogue beliefs at work in your heart right now? In what ways have they betrayed you?
3. In your struggle with sin, how have you pursued God's wisdom? How have you fallen short in your pursuit of truth?
4. Which ruling desires most often ascend the throne of your heart?
5. Which false beliefs most often fuel your diehard sins?
6. What will you begin doing right now to take inventory of the beliefs and wants that are at work in your heart?

PART 3

Bring Christ and His
Provisions to Your Fight

Andrea's Diehard Sin

In a grade-school performance of *Alice in Wonderland*, Andrea played the part of the White Rabbit. "I'm late! I'm late! For a very important date!" In nearly prophetic fashion, her grade-school role has become her adult persona. Andrea has many important places to be and people to see, but no matter where she is supposed to be or who she is scheduled to meet, she is always late.

Maybe you are taking offense here. "Oh, so it's a sin to be late?! Where is that in the Bible?" It's true—there is no command in the Bible that says, "Thou shalt not be tardy." But we have various and sundry commands to love our neighbors. Christlike love is not rude or selfish (see 1 Cor. 13:5–7). Andrea habitually runs thirty minutes behind her own schedule and the schedule of others, leaving them floating in a wake of wasted time.

On the surface, it's clear that Andrea's problem with lateness is complicated by an ongoing struggle with time management and a compulsion to cram her schedule with more and more. And while guarding her schedule will certainly help her, there's a more spiritual area that she needs to change: Andrea values her own agenda and accomplishments over the interests of other people. In this, she fails to love them well—and unless she begins to love her neighbor as herself, Andrea will be perpetually cast as the White Rabbit.

8

Opening the Vaults of Gospel Treasure

*The King, full of mercy and goodness, very far from chastising
me, embraces me with love, makes me eat at His table, serves
me with His own hands, gives me the key of His treasures.*
BROTHER LAWRENCE (1614–1691)

The Sree Padmanabhaswamy Temple is the richest temple in
the world. Highly treasured among the people of Kerala in
India, the Hindu temple glimmers with solid gold walls and
shrines to various deities. But its millions of annual visitors
didn't know the half of it until 2011, when a treasury audit
approved the unsealing of seven treasure vaults stuffed with
golden elephants, idols draped in diamond chains, bags of gold
coins, ornate crowns, and sixty-six-pound gold coconut shells
set with precious stones.

Since then, another secret room—Chamber B—was found
hidden behind two enormous gold doors embossed with fierce
golden cobras. Auditors estimate that this hidden vault could
bring the total value of Padmanabhaswamy Temple beyond
one trillion rupees (over $15 billion)![1] The chamber doors

---

1. Malavika Bhattacharya, *The Rough Guide to India*, 10th ed. (London: Rough
Guides, 2016), 1044–46.

remain sealed shut as superstition, fear, tradition, and red tape threaten to keep these unknown riches shrouded in mystery. Even from my house, 9,000 miles away, I want to know what wondrous discoveries await in Chamber B.

A Gospel Full of Gospel Blessings

Even as they admired the temple's regal architecture, millions of residents and visitors were oblivious to the full extent of the vast riches surrounding them. Similarly, the gospel is a glorious monument to the sovereignty, wisdom, and goodness of God, yet no Christian has truly estimated the infinite riches contained within its walls. This observation is not as much a critique of our weakness as it is an exaltation of the gospel's surpassing value.

To put it bluntly, no one fully grasps the gospel. No one knows how high and wide and deep our gospel fortunes run. We admire the gospel, and over time we develop a better appreciation for our Lord and His life-changing good news. But even the most spiritually insightful men and women of our churches fall short of accounting for the vast and marvelous blessings that belong to us by faith in Christ. Indeed, the gospel is exceedingly valuable!

Vault after vault of grace-infused provisions are ours by faith in Christ. How will you seek out a deeper appreciation of Christ and His work for you? As you become more aware of the riches that He gives, what will you do with the treasures you discover in the gospel?

The gospel is good news that delivers immeasurable spiritual blessings from God's hand. Nothing in this world compares to the abounding grace that flows to us through the glorious message of Christian redemption. Paul delighted in God's call to spread the gospel and declared, "How beautiful are the feet of those who bring good news of good things!" (Rom. 10:15). Mark this: Paul did not only say that he and his fellow evangelists were bringing good news in a generic sense. Rather he pointed out that they brought to weary and wayward souls a gospel full of good things.

The book of Isaiah shows us some of the good things that Paul declared through the gospel. Here in Romans, Paul is actually quoting Isaiah, who himself wrote, "How lovely on the mountains are the feet of him who brings good news, who announces peace and brings good news of happiness, who announces salvation, and says to Zion, 'Your God reigns!'" (Isa. 52:7). What good things belong to those who hear with faith the good news of Jesus? Through the gospel we have peace with God, lasting joy, full salvation, and the exhilarating promise that our God is in control. I believe that this only begins to scratch the surface of the good things we receive as heirs of God's kingdom.

If you were heir to a similar earthly inheritance, how would you handle it? Would you stash away your treasure and forget about it? Would you squander your resources? Would you entrust the riches to untrustworthy stewards? Of course no one in his right mind would treat an inheritance in these ways. But you and I do often neglect the many gospel blessings that come to us through faith in Jesus. As a result, our hearts are tempted to look elsewhere for the help that we need. To help you to leverage your gospel riches against the enemy of sin, a detailed plan is awaiting you in appendix A.

Counterfeit Solutions

The vast riches of Padmanabhaswamy Temple were in danger of not only remaining hidden, but also being stolen. When the mysterious vaults were unsealed, officials were alarmed by the discovery of a gold-plating machine and an underground

tunnel. They regretfully concluded that thieves had been pil-
fering the priceless temple treasures and leaving counterfeit
replicas in their places. I see in this another insightful picture
of our struggle to truly embrace the gospel in daily life. As long
as we are unaware of the gospel blessings that Christ purchased
for us, the world, the flesh, and the devil conspire together to
offer us a series of counterfeit alternatives. The deceptive pull
of self-help secrets, bankrupt secular psychologies, and empty
philosophies of men allure us. Instead of dismissing fraudulent
solutions out of hand, we allow our spiritual inheritance to
be pilfered and replaced with counterfeits. Eliza fell prey to
the sinful practice of gossip through its counterfeit promise
of self-righteousness. Instead of resting securely in the righteousness of Christ, she exalted herself by slandering others.
Paul warned his first-century hearers about the danger of being
captivated by false promises: "See to it that no one takes you
captive through philosophy and empty deception, according
to the tradition of men, according to the elementary principles
of the world, rather than according to Christ" (Col. 2:8).

Writing to the believers of Colossae, Paul delivered the
astounding truth that in Christ are hidden "all the treasures of
wisdom and knowledge" (Col. 2:3). What makes this declaration so incredible is the word *all*. Christ does not possess some
wisdom and knowledge—all wisdom and knowledge belong
to Him. Spiritual explorers may scour the universe in search of
truth, but apart from Christ they return empty-handed. Furthermore, Paul also taught us that all of God's promises are yes in
Christ (see 2 Cor. 1:20). Combine the golden treasures of all the
vaults known to man, and their sum will pale in comparison to
the surpassing value of knowing Christ (see Phil. 3:8). In a million lifetimes we could not explore all that the Lord Jesus is for
us and all that He brings to us. And yet knowing that His riches
are unsearchable motivates us to seek them out all the more.

As we prepare to overcome our diehard sin habits, we will uncover five major provisions that are granted to us in Christ, which we must learn to bring into our daily spiritual battles. As God calls us to bear good fruit, we must extend our roots into His stream of grace. The spiritual resources that we will consider over the rest of this chapter and into chapter nine are God Himself, the Bible, the gospel, the church, and the ordinances. Within each, you will find practical instruction for extending your roots and bearing good fruits through the powerful resources that we have in Christ.

The Provision of God Himself

Ironically, as we take inventory of Christ's provisions, we frequently overlook the most important provision of all. In our daily lives, we often give thanks to God for the many good gifts that He gives to us or the wonderful works that He does in our lives. But how often we overlook the ultimate gift: God Himself.

Through His redemptive work announced in the gospel, the startling reality is revealed to us: our triune God sent Himself into our miserable world to care for our souls. He did not send down a program for us to follow—although His Scriptures do contain the words of life. He did not send a delegation of angels to die on our behalf—although that would be a significant sacrifice. He did not send a specially trained human to negotiate with us on His behalf—although He certainly does use wise people to turn us back to Him. No; instead, our triune God sent Himself. God the Father sent His very own Son to enter our world and redeem us (see Gal. 4:4).

The Nicene Creed reminds us that the God-man entered our world through the miracle of incarnation—"the only Son of God, begotten from the Father before all ages, God from God, Light from Light, true God from true God, begotten, not made; of the same essence as the Father." He lived a perfect life in our place, died a sacrificial death because of our sin, and triumphantly rose from the grave as our hope of glory. Then, after His ascension to the right hand of God the Father, God sent Himself again. He sent His promised Holy Spirit—the third divine person of the Trinity—as our Comforter who would lead us into all truth and sustain us until Jesus returns again. How do we so easily miss this invaluable reality of the Christian life? Through the gospel, God gave us Himself. This changes every aspect of life—especially how we wage war against ongoing sin.

A right understanding of God's presence should affect our battles with sin in many ways. Primarily, though, it will assure us that we are never alone in the fight. This one small truth has made many big differences in my life and ministry. I remember when it suddenly dawned on my heart. *He's here with me*, I thought to myself. *He's alive and here right now, by His Spirit, working for my good.* Meditating on the reality of God's kindness—His entering my world, securing my salvation, drawing me to Himself, pledging to me His perfecting love, and caring for me in the present moments of life—transformed the way that I view my situations and the situations of others.

Whenever I come alongside fellow believers, I remind them that Jesus is a living Savior who is present with us in our trouble. He fights alongside us, through us, and for us. We can fight against sin because it is God who is at work in us, both to will and to work for His good pleasure (Phil. 2:13).

When preaching the gospel to myself, I have learned to firmly impress on my own soul the glorious proximity of Jesus, who is risen, present, at work, and returning.[2] "The most holy and necessary practice in our spiritual life is the presence of

---

2. David Powlison, *Seeing with New Eyes: Counseling and the Human Condition Through the Lens of Scripture* (Phillipsburg, NJ: P&R, 2003), 43.

God," wrote the fifteenth-century monk Brother Lawrence. "That means finding constant pleasure in His divine company, speaking humbly and lovingly with Him in all seasons, at every moment, without limiting the conversation in any way."[3] If we will make progress against the diehard sin habits that plague us, the first of Christ's provisions that we need to bring into our situation is God Himself.

The Provision of the Bible

God has ordained that His Word factor prominently in the life of every person He helps. Just as Jesus is His chosen Redeemer, the Bible is His chosen instrument, and God's Spirit uses it to bring change. King David exalts Scripture as the all-sufficient resource for life change when he writes,

> The law of the LORD is perfect, restoring the soul;
> The testimony of the LORD is sure, making wise the simple.
> The precepts of the LORD are right, rejoicing the heart;
> The commandment of the LORD is pure, enlightening the eyes.
> The fear of the LORD is clean, enduring forever;
> The judgments of the LORD are true; they are righteous
>   altogether.
> They are more desirable than gold, yes, than much fine gold;
> Sweeter also than honey and the drippings of the honeycomb.
> Moreover, by them Your servant is warned;
> In keeping them there is great reward. (Ps. 19:7–11)

Notice the words that David uses. The Bible is *perfect, sure, right, pure, clean, true, righteous, desirable,* and *sweet.* As the

---

3. Brother Lawrence, *Spiritual Maxims of Brother Lawrence* (New York: Simon and Schuster, 2013), 6.

Spirit of God ministers His truth to our souls, our hearts and lives are progressively transformed. Scripture restores the soul, makes people wise, rejoices the heart, enlightens the eyes, endures forever, warns of danger, and delivers a great reward. The Word of God is sufficient for our every need.

God is certainly able to change the lives of people who disregard His Scriptures—the sovereign God does whatever He pleases. However, people who neglect reading God's Word, knowing it, and applying it to their lives should not expect their struggles with sin to improve. We must intentionally fight sin with Scripture. Let's briefly consider the ways we can do this.

Bible Reading

Nehemiah publicly read from the Scriptures from early morning until midday, and all the people were attentive to the book of the law (see Neh. 8:3). We should do all that we can to bring to bear this distinct commitment to reading the Bible in our own lives. I'm not suggesting that you spend the first four or five hours of each day reading the Bible (although from time to time this practice would certainly bear fruit). What I am suggesting is that you consider the role of simple Bible reading in your daily walk with Christ.

Are you reading the Bible every day (or nearly every day)? Do you have a plan for keeping up with this important discipline? To fight wisely against daily sin habits, you need to be regularly nourished on the words of God. You need to hear again and again God's promises to you, His instructions for life, what pleases and grieves Him. Regular Bible reading will also keep your heart tuned to His will, so that you might be ready to resist temptation and pursue holiness.

A variety of Bible-reading plans are available online. For the average reader, daily readings will take about thirty minutes to complete. If you are new to Bible reading, let me encourage you to get moving as soon as possible. You might even consider closing this book and reading the Bible right now. You can always find your place in this book again later.

Bible Meditation

Reading the Bible is an essential part of feeding on the truth, but reading alone is not enough. If we aren't careful, Bible reading can become a mindless routine. But if we apply the discipline of meditation to our Bible reading, its takeaway value dramatically increases.

In Psalm 119, a 176-verse psalm that magnifies the Word of God, we read about the importance of meditation.

> I will meditate on Your precepts
> And regard Your ways.
> I shall delight in Your statutes;
> I shall not forget Your word. (Ps. 119:15–16)

Whereas regular reading of the Bible builds our knowledge of Scripture, meditation builds our understanding of Scripture.

What is meditation? Puritan Thomas Hooker describes it as "a serious intention of the mind whereby we come to search out the truth, and settle it effectually upon the heart."[4] Meditating on Scripture requires us to slow down and focus on a particular portion of God's Word, which is a valuable practice in the fight against sin. Replacing sin habits with habits of holiness requires focused attention on the truth and consistent practice. It is never enough to eliminate an ungodly habit. The habit must be replaced instead. We form new habits by practicing the new patterns for living that God has shown us in His Word.

---

4. Quoted in Perry Miller and Thomas H. Johnson, eds., *The Puritans: A Sourcebook of Their Writings* (Mineola, NY: Dover Publications, 2001), 301.

Therefore, patiently meditating on Scripture is a foundational part of replacing sinful patterns with new patterns of godliness.

We fight our diehard sins by gaining a true understanding of our spiritual needs. Armed with this knowledge, we are able to meditate on specific Scriptures that are directed at a particular sin habit. Meditation allows us to precisely apply Scripture to the problem we are facing.

Earlier we were introduced to Carl, who struggled to escape the sin of laziness. Above all, Carl needed the Word of God to settle into his heart and establish new standards of living for God's glory. To fight against this diehard sin, Carl set his mind to meditating on key passages of Scripture such as Ephesians 4:28: "He who steals must steal no longer; but rather he must labor, performing with his own hands what is good, so that he will have something to share with one who has need." Through faithful meditation on Scripture, Carl became convinced of his need for change, then learned new ways of living to the glory of God. As Carl prayerfully meditated on God's perspective on laziness and apathy, the Holy Spirit enlightened his mind to learn how to put off sin and put on righteousness.

Scripture presents this put off / put on dynamic as a central aspect of the process of change. Paul says, "Lay aside the old self, which is being corrupted in accordance with the lusts of deceit, and . . . put on the new self, which in the likeness of God has been created in righteousness and holiness of the truth" (Eph. 4:22–24). The Bible is sufficient to instruct us about specific sinful ways of living that we need to put off, as well as about the corresponding replacements to put on. We should not assume that we can decide, on our own, what changes are needed in our lives. God has ordained Scripture as the instruction manual for killing sin. Thus we should take the Word of God seriously through meditation, so that we will know what and how to change.

Bible Memorization

Knowing God's Word by heart gives us immediate recall of the wise counsel we need in order to fight sin. Remember that "the good man out of the good treasure of his heart brings forth what is good; and the evil man out of the evil treasure brings forth what is evil" (Luke 6:45). The good man has the good deposit of gospel truth planted in his heart. As he meditates on divine truth, his heart and life are continually conformed to the image of Christ.

To assist you in Scripture memorization, let me share a little-known secret. The best kind of memorization is that which comes through consistent meditation. Early in my Christian life, I made a critical error. I worked out my Scripture memory muscles for only a brief time in the morning. Soon afterward, I had already forgotten what I had hoped to learn by heart. But I wised up after finding the secret to memorizing Scripture. The Bible told me that people who walk with God delight in His law by meditating on it day and night (see Ps. 1:2). In other words, the secret to knowing God's Word is an unbroken chain of meditated moments. The Puritans called this "redeeming the time."[5]

We redeem the time by capturing those little moments that we know are slipping away in the normal course of life—when our minds are idling while we lay awake in bed, scrub the dishes, shuttle the kids, mow the lawn, and complete a host of other necessary tasks. When we allow these valuable moments to slip idly by, our minds are free to wander back into our old

---

5. They learned this from the Bible, too: "Be careful how you walk, not as unwise men but as wise, making the most of your time, because the days are evil" (Eph. 5:15–16). On the basis of this truth, Pastor Jonathan Edwards resolved "never to lose one moment of time; but improve it the most profitable way I possibly can" (quoted in Steven J. Lawson, *The Unwavering Resolve of Jonathan Edwards* [Lake Mary, FL: Reformation Trust, 2008], 95, 158). As with all resolutions, it's important to remember that all our efforts are motivated and empowered by God's grace.

patterns of thinking. This practice of redeeming these moments is an essential part of the plan for resisting temptation and sin. If we are not ready to quickly bring Scripture to mind, our ability to replace temptation with Scripture will wane.

We are resolved to redeem the time not because God is standing over us in wrath but because He is walking with us by grace. Are you motivated to memorize the Word of God? Start today. Find a passage of Scripture that speaks to your struggle and begin prayerfully working to see it written on the tablet of your heart.

Bible Study

The faithful Christian who fights valiantly against the die-hard sins of life will inevitably be a diligent student of God's Word. Make a list in your mind of the Christians who you admire most. If your list is anything like mine, every person is a thoughtful Bible learner. We too must follow their example of reading, meditating on, memorizing, and studying Scripture.

These important spiritual disciplines belong to all of us— not just those we consider to be giants of the faith. Andrea, who perpetually ran late, heeded her friend's encouragement to slow down and reconsider her priorities. As she hustled around from morning until night, the priority of God's Word had faded into the background of her life. Convicted, Andrea renewed her commitment to the Bible. A refreshing season of daily reading awakened in her heart a love for Bible meditation and memorization. The nourishment that she gained and the changes that God worked in her life drove her to an even closer study of Scripture that helped her to minister to others.

Using study tools such as Bible commentaries, dictionaries, and lexicons are helpful, but at the heart of effective Bible study is simply a desire to know God by spending thoughtful time in His Word. If you are not familiar with the more intense tools of Bible study, you can still learn much by listening to wise preaching, reading the study notes in your Bible, and discussing what you learn with other believers who share your desire to gain strength for fighting sin, endurance for running with Christ, and wisdom for bearing fruit to His glory.

Getting Serious about Change

On pages 185–87 of Appendix A, I've provided more practical steps for putting these provisions to work in your life. Turn there now to get started.

Janet's Diehard Sin

Everywhere Janet goes, she feels guilty. Like John Bunyan's Christian pilgrim, she slumps under the weight of her burden. Regardless of what she does or how her friends encourage her, Janet's closest companion is a low-grade feeling of shame. Even when spirits run high at a party that is thrown in her honor, she feels like a loser. The failures of her youth haunt her at the age of fifty-eight, and her continual shortcomings at work and at home torment her. Guilt drives her hard. She obsesses over trivial decisions, afraid of making a bad choice. When her children sin, she blames herself. The first and most frequent phrase from her lips is "I'm sorry." Janet is a slave to her guilty conscience, and it shows in her life. But what's going on beneath the surface, amid the roots of her heart? What beliefs are at the center of her slavery to guilt?

9

Nourishing Our Souls

I know One who suffered and made satisfaction [on] my behalf.
MARTIN LUTHER (1483–1546)

According to Jeremiah, there are only two ways we can live: as a desert bush or as a fruit tree (see Jer. 17:5–8). The blessed, or happy, man is he who trusts implicitly in the Lord and bears good fruit as a result. Unlike the cursed man, who trusts in himself and in his own strength, the man who is blessed turns his heart toward the Lord, not away from Him. He is nourished by a life-giving stream—an oasis in a dry and weary land where otherwise there is no water. The blessed man flourishes even in an oppressive year of heat and drought, while the cursed man's self-trusting nature puts him in a dry, stony land—a place of death.

Jeremiah's stream reminds us of the redeeming, sanctifying, and enabling grace that flows from Christ to each of His covenant people. If our own lives are to reflect the blessed man of Jeremiah 17, we too must extend our roots by the stream of God's provisions that are secured in Christ, applied by the Spirit, and revealed to us in Scripture. By keeping our hearts rooted in His grace, we are slowly transformed—drawn away from the old lives we lived apart from Christ and conformed to the new life and worldview that we received by faith in Him.

Though we once bore the thorns of sin and were ruled by rogue desires and false beliefs, we now, nourished by His stream of grace, learn to follow godly desires and true beliefs.

The Provision of the Gospel

No message is more central to the Christian life than the good news of Jesus Christ. It is the heartbeat, the lifeblood, the spirit and soul of our walks with Christ. Paul described the gospel message as that which was "of first importance" (1 Cor. 15:3). Yet the gospel is often misunderstood, so we ought to start with what the gospel is *not*.

The gospel is not a style of music. Southern gospel melodies and lyrics have a way of boiling down biblical truth to its essence and dressing it in a comforting tune. The down-to-earth simplicity appeals to those with ears to hear. But while gospel music certainly can communicate the good news of Christ, the gospel is far more than a musical genre.

The gospel is not a book. Although we call the first four books of the New Testament—Matthew, Mark, Luke, and John—the Gospels, the gospel is not merely a historical account of the words and works of Jesus. When Paul confesses, "I am not ashamed of the gospel," he does not mean that he is proud of the four red-lettered records of Jesus's earthly life and ministry (Rom. 1:16). These works do contain the gospel message, but they are not the gospel.

The gospel is not a scheme for material gain. The "prosperity gospel" is no gospel at all. This false teaching offers helpless people a false Jesus as their false savior. Though the true gospel is heralded as the announcement of divine favor toward the elect, never does the Bible promise our best life now. The real gospel is infinitely better. It promises joy and hope even in the absence of worldly gain. God's people exalt in the Lord,

Though the fig tree should not blossom
And there be no fruit on the vines,
Though the yield of the olive should fail
And the fields produce no food,
Though the flock should be cut off from the fold
And there be no cattle in the stalls. (Hab. 3:17–18)

The gospel is not a lifestyle. We often hear preaching and teaching that exhorts Christians to "live the gospel." There is a good intention here of motivating people to care so much about the gospel that it influences every area of their lives. However, the gospel is not livable—it is not something that we are called to do.[1] Rather it is a life-giving message of Jesus—how He lived, how He died, and how He rose again for us.

The gospel is not a law. Throughout Scripture, the law presents to us God's righteous judgments, requirements, commands, and expectations. In His law, God reveals His perfect, holy character. The law is good. However, we are not good. Therefore, the good law of God delivers bad news to us. Like a hammer, the law crashes down on us. We must not confuse the gospel for a second-chance law that will rescue us if we just keep it. The gospel doesn't command us to do anything. Rather, the gospel is about Christ and what He has accomplished on our behalf through His eternal plan of redemption.

The Good News

The gospel is a glorious, heralded announcement of good news to those who need it most. Infused by God with illuminating power, the gospel of grace softens our hearts and

1. Please hear me when I say that we don't need to correct our brothers and sisters every time we hear an entreaty to "live out the gospel." We most certainly are called to flood our lives with the many good gifts that come to us because of the good news.

brings us to Christ by faith. Beyond His work of converting us through the gospel, God also motivates us to holy living through the gospel. We once were enslaved to sin; the gospel has set us free to be new creatures in Christ (see 2 Cor. 5:17). Following Christ is a gospel-centered experience from beginning to end. We come into Christ by hearing the gospel with faith, and we grow up into Christ by continually hearing the gospel with faith.

The apostle Paul warned the Galatian Christians against pursuing holiness by works of the law rather than by the transforming power of the gospel (see Gal. 3:5). The gospel is the central, empowering resource for fighting sin. It motivates us to holiness in three ways.

The gospel gives us a better goal than merely coping. Much of the self-help section in the local Christian bookstore aims for life management. But through the powerful working of the gospel, Christ offers us lasting biblical change. Rather than coping strategies, we have in the gospel a promise of true transformation.

The gospel gives us a new affection. Apart from Christ, our affections and desires are disordered. We chase after an endless string of hopes and dreams that can never truly satisfy. But when the gospel breaks through, our old affections are expelled by a new affection for the glory of God and His soul-satisfying goodness.

The gospel gives us a true hero to follow. I often catch myself daydreaming, and I'm embarrassed to admit that my daydreams often include scenes of chaos and danger. As each scene plays out, a hero swoops in to settle the chaos, disarm the danger, and sort out the confusion. Can you guess who is the hero of my daydreams? Me. Oh what delusions of grandeur rule my heart! But in the gospel, an infinitely more wonderful hero rules—not only in the made-up world of my mind, but also in the fallen, real world. The gospel offers us a better hero, and by hearing His good news announced over and over again we gain hope and help so that we can change in real and meaningful ways.

Preaching the Gospel to Ourselves

Every Christian must grow to apply Christ and His answers to his or her own trials, temptations, and sin troubles. This kind of personal soul care signals you to do something called *preaching the gospel to yourself.*[2] This means "that you continually face up to your own sinfulness and then flee to Jesus through faith in His shed blood and righteous life. It means that you appropriate, again by faith, the fact that Jesus fully satisfied the law of God, that He is your propitiation, and that God's holy wrath is no longer directed toward you."[3]

Everything that I've presented up to this point has been, essentially, leading us to do this. But the question remains: How exactly do we minister the surpassing riches of God's grace to our own souls? How do we bring Christ and His solutions to bear on our diehard sins? How do we preach the gospel to ourselves?

Know the difference between the law and the gospel. "Distinguishing between the Law and the Gospel is the highest art in Christendom, one that every person who values the name

2. Jerry Bridges, *The Discipline of Grace: God's Role and Our Role in the Pursuit of Holiness* (Colorado Springs: NavPress, 2006), 8. Jerry Bridges credits Jack Miller, former professor at Westminster Seminary, with popularizing the expression "Preach the gospel to yourself every day."

3. Bridges, 59.

Christian ought to recognize, know, and possess," said the gospel-loving reformer Martin Luther.[4] The relationship between the law and the gospel is one of immense importance to us in our fight against sin. Mistaking the law for the gospel sets us on an unhelpful trajectory toward a legalistic Christian life, in which we relate to God on the basis of our works. However, mistaking the gospel for the law sets us on an equally unhelpful trajectory toward lawlessness in the Christian life, in which we relate to God as though obedience to His commands were unimportant.

Recognizing the difference between the voice of the law and the voice of the gospel is a daily task for the sin-killing Christian. In simple terms, the law says, "Do this and you may live." The law offers a promise of life to those who remain in good standing through perfect obedience to God's commands. As you can imagine, "Do this and live" is exceedingly bad news to people who have not kept God's standard.[5] The law drives the sinner to despair and leaves him without hope. The law cannot save; it can only light the path of obedience and condemn all who stray from it.

The gospel, however, frees us to live and obey. Ralph Erskine writes, "A rigid matter was the law, demanding brick, denying straw, but when with gospel tongue it sings, it bids me fly and gives me wings."[6] Where the law says, "Do this and live," the gospel brings a better word: "Live!" The gospel calls

4. Martin Luther, "The Distinction Between the Law and the Gospel" (sermon, January 1, 1532), trans. Willard Burce, in *Concordia Journal* 18 (April 1992): 153.

5. "Thus it is, that the freer the Gospel, the more sanctifying is the Gospel; and the more it is received as a doctrine of grace, the more will it be felt as a doctrine according to godliness. This is one of the secrets of the Christian life, that the more a man holds of God as a pensioner, the greater is the payment of service that he renders back again. On the tenure of 'Do this and live,' a spirit of fearfulness is sure to enter" (Thomas Chalmers, "The Expulsive Power of a New Affection," in *The Works of Thomas Chalmers, D. D.* [Philadelphia, 1833], 387).

6. *The Sermons and Practical Works of Ralph Erskine* (Glasgow, 1778), 10:283.

us from the grave of sin. It grants us life—not on the basis of our law keeping but on the perfect obedience of Christ. Through the gospel, God gives saving grace to convert our dead, cold hearts. And once we are alive, God continues to give us, through the gospel, enabling grace to honor His law.

Have a keenly attentive ear. You must learn to listen to the messages that are moving in and out of your heart. And you must learn to speak truth to yourself. Dr. Martyn Lloyd-Jones asks, "Have you realized that most of your unhappiness in life is due to the fact that you are listening to yourself instead of talking to yourself?"[7] A Christian who cares about holiness will often hear the condemning voice of the law. If you lean toward legalism, you may find yourself tempted to ramp up your good deeds as a countermeasure to your continued sin. If you lean toward licentiousness, you may be tempted to silence the voice of the law that calls attention to your sin struggle. Both responses are unwise. The proper response to the demanding voice of the law is to preach the good news to yourself first. Then you will have the power necessary to obey.

Gospel First, Change Second

You look into the law of God as a mirror and see the ugliness of your sin reflected back at you. As someone who wants to love and please God, you feel the reality of your sin stirring up in you both discouragement and a fierce desire to change. You recommit yourself to stop sinning and to start living right. You open the Bible in search of which dos and don'ts will solve your sin problem. You lace up your spiritual gloves and start swinging at your sin, but you feel as though you are beating

7. D. Martyn Lloyd-Jones, *Spiritual Depression: Its Causes and Its Cure* (Grand Rapids: Eerdmans, 1965), 20.

the air. You pant and sweat, but little change results. What's missing?

There is an order to living the Christian life: gospel first, change second. When God's convicting influence alerts us to any wayward habit in our lives, a routine temptation follows closely behind. It is the temptation to shape up and get with the program. While a resolute desire to change is essential to killing sin, it is not the first step. The gospel must come first, or else we will flounder in our self-empowered efforts.

The Bible routinely displays this fundamental order of things. God indicates His gospel promise to Abraham, and then Abraham obeys (see Gen. 12:1–4). John recounts that we come to love God in response to God's declaration of love for us (see 1 John 4:19). The most striking example of this life-giving, one-two punch can be seen in the letter to the Romans, as Paul gives not one command in the first five chapters. Across the first third of the letter, Paul floods every page with the gospel: who Christ is in us, what He has done for us, how He ministers grace to us. The first command does not appear until Romans 6—and what an astounding command we find! "Even so consider yourselves to be dead to sin, but alive to God in Christ Jesus" (Rom. 6:11).

If killing sin was important to Paul, why didn't he write this in the first line, in all caps? "Paul, a bondservant of Christ, etc.: STOP SINNING!" Paul knew personally that the gospel alone contains the power we need in order to obey God's law. Therefore, in his magnum opus, Paul preached the gospel across 148 verses before giving his first command. There is no mistaking the importance of this order.

There are actually two mirrors in Scripture: the law and the gospel. Martin Luther wrote, "The highest of all God's commands is this, that we hold up before our eyes the image of his dear Son, our Lord Jesus Christ."[8] Before you can look with hope at your sin through the mirror of the law, you must look at Christ through the mirror of His gospel. When kept in the proper order, both the law and the gospel work together to comfort and direct us in the Christian life as we fight valiantly to kill sin.

The Provision of the Church

While it is true that God elects, calls, saves, and keeps individual people, it is also true that every individual Christian is part of a larger body of believers called the church. In Christ, we are all brothers and sisters who together are heirs of His righteousness. By blood—the blood of Christ—we belong to one another. As Eve was given to Adam as a support and help, all of us have been knit together in Christ to care for one another.

Teaching the Ephesian believers about God's gifting within the church, Paul explained why God outfits each of His chosen people with various abilities. These gifts are

> for the equipping of the saints for the work of service, to the building up of the body of Christ; until we all attain to the unity of the faith, and of the knowledge of the Son of God, to a mature man, to the measure of the stature which belongs to the fullness of Christ. (Eph. 4:12–13)

Notice that when dearly loved followers of Christ use their gifts, His body is built up in the faith. Each member grows

---

8. He continues, "Every day he should be our excellent mirror wherein we behold how much God loves us and how well, in his infinite goodness, he has cared for us in that he gave his dear Son for us. . . . Do not let this mirror and throne of grace be torn away from before your eyes" (quoted in Theodore G. Tappert, ed. and trans., *Luther: Letters of Spiritual Counsel* [1960; repr., Vancouver: Regent College Publishing, 2003], 116).

into the stature—or maturity—of Christ's fullness. They grow up into Christ. In the following verses of Ephesians 4, Paul goes on to explain that the church is built up by love, as its members mutually minister the truth to one another. True believers commit themselves to mutual ministry, spiritually caring for each other in a variety of ways.

Prayer

God has ordained prayer as a special means by which He accomplishes His plans. His people minister to one another by prayer. If you have a prayer list already, I expect that it includes items such as physical needs to be met, circumstances to be changed, or worrisome expectations to be brought to a happy conclusion. All of these and more should find a place on our prayer agendas.

What about prayers for killing sin? We pray for the death of sin in our own lives—but do we pray the same for other people? James says, "Confess your sins to one another, and pray for one another so that you may be healed. The effective prayer of a righteous man can accomplish much" (James 5:16). The second part of this verse is most familiar. We happily anticipate the powerful results of righteous prayer. But we must not overlook the concern for sin that James clearly envisions within the content of these prayers.

What do righteous people pray about for each other? We pray about our mutual struggles with sin. Confess your sins to one another and pray, James says. This kind of intercession seems lost on many Christians, and it's understandable. Transparency about our sin is difficult. It requires a mutual trust to be forged in biblical brotherhood and sisterhood. God has ordained the covenant community of the church as the place where people share a common desire for spiritual change and wield the powerful weapon of prayer on behalf of one another.

Do you belong to a church in which people are willing to talk about their sin and confidentially pray for one another?

Encouragement

In popular culture, the idea of encouragement has lost much of its punch. The word brings to mind a well-timed compliment, the "Attaboy" that a child receives for doing a chore around the house, or an effort to nudge someone toward a good decision. But biblical encouragement is far more powerful. The biblical word[9] calls to mind two people coming alongside each other and walking together through the ups and downs of life. In the Bible we are commanded to "encourage one another and build up one another" (1 Thess. 5:11). In particular, this includes lovingly encouraging one another to put away difficult sin habits.

God created us to live in community as we pursue lasting biblical change in our lives and make much of Christ in the world. Scripture exhorts us, as people who know the reality of sin as well as the future hope that we have in Christ, to walk with one another in uniquely encouraging ways. In the context of faithful and healthy local churches, we gather together for mutual encouragement. Are you cultivating relationships in which other people have freedom to personally encourage you to put off sin and put on holiness?

Counsel

The church is also ordained by God to be the source of godly counsel. David Powlison writes, "The Lord's people are called to help each other grow up. We are called to know and be known by each other. We are called to counsel each other,

---

9. *Parakaleo.* God most commonly uses this word to describe the advocacy and help of the Holy Spirit—He is the Paraclete.

to be change agents in each other's lives."[10] Every believer is a counselor, and every healthy church is a counseling ministry.

Does that sound like a strange way to talk about the church? We usually think of counseling in terms of the professional help of the psychiatrist's couch. In reality, counsel is simply the communication of instructions for life. There are only two kinds of instruction: the counsel of the godly and the counsel of the wicked (see Ps. 1). The question is not whether or not we are counselors. The question is, What kind of counselors are we?

Of course, particularly difficult issues often arise in the lives of other people, and we feel inadequate to give meaningful counsel. However, this is no reason for us to shrink back; rather, it is an opportunity for us to connect with a pastor or biblical counselor who has more experience and wisdom so that we can become more competent in our own ability to counsel the word. True counsel belongs to the church, because God has made His people the stewards of sanctifying truth. We counsel each other in two main ways.

The people of God use words to counsel the truth to one another. Timothy heard Paul's command to

> retain the standard of sound words which you have heard from me, in the faith and love which are in Christ Jesus. Guard, through the Holy Spirit who dwells in us, the treasure which has been entrusted to you. (2 Tim. 1:13–14)

Every believer is entrusted with the privilege and responsibility of guarding the truth that God has revealed in His world and,

---

10. David Powlison, *Speaking Truth in Love: Counsel in Community* (Greensboro, NC: New Growth Press, 2005), 99.

most importantly, in His Word. But, like faithful stewards, we don't hide the truth in the ground where it cannot be maligned (see Matt. 25:18). Instead, we put the truth to work in our own lives and in the lives of other people.

The people of God also minister God's grace to one another by their examples. They model godly thoughts, words, and actions. Paul considered himself to be an example of how to pursue Christ. He then encouraged Timothy to "let no one look down on your youthfulness, but rather in speech, conduct, love, faith and purity, show yourself an example of those who believe" (1 Tim. 4:12). Even as a younger member of Christ's body, Timothy was to be a helpful example to others. Furthermore, Christians minister God's grace to one another through their presence in one another's lives. Throughout the early church, suffering and sinning believers were comforted when others arrived to care for them in Christ-centered ways.

Healthy churches are places where godly counsel thrives in the lives of people. Members of the church, which Jesus has promised to build, should seek out opportunities for personal ministry to one another as godly counselors. While the counsel of the wicked leads to sin's growth, the counsel of the godly strikes at the root of sin, helping us to put our sin habits to death. The church, then, is another key provision that God has given us in Christ to help us combat diehard sin habits. In this short space, we have considered a number of points about how the people of God can help one another to fight the good fight. There is more to be said for the church's role in killing sin. In the next chapter, we will consider a few more points about fighting sin as a community of believers.

The Provision of the Ordinances

Have you ever thought of baptism and the Lord's Supper as spiritual helps against stubborn sin? Truth be told, these ordinances are not only means of giving worship to God. They are also means of God's grace toward us. Although we are not saved by being baptized or by taking the elements of communion, both are means of God's sanctifying grace—they help us to know, love, and follow Christ. Reflecting regularly on baptism and the Lord's Supper gives us two more prime opportunities to feed our souls. By the work of God's Spirit, the gospel message is vibrant and active in both of these sacraments. How do they help us?

As Testimonies

Baptism and the Lord's Supper contain testimonies of God's comprehensive care for our souls. In baptism, testimonies of our cleansing, repentance, and union with Christ are present.[11] We invite believers and unbelievers to attend our church's baptism services because we know that God often grants His good gifts to those who behold with faith the picture of the gospel displayed in water baptism.

The Lord's Supper also serves as a testimony of God's grace in the death of His Son. The bread symbolizes His body, broken for us. The fruit of the vine symbolizes the sin-forgiving blood of Christ, shed on the cross. Paul reminded the church at Corinth, "As often as you eat this bread and drink the cup, you proclaim the Lord's death until He comes" (1 Cor. 11:26).

Faithful churches will fence the table, asking any unbelievers who are present at the time to refrain from participating in

11. John M. Frame, *Systematic Theology: An Introduction to Christian Belief* (Phillipsburg, NJ: P&R, 2013), 1062.

communion. Nevertheless, most churches welcome unbelievers to observe it, because the testimony of the gospel is again clear, as it is in baptism. This powerful testimony of the gospel is not only for unbelievers. It is also an important tool of God in your life.

As Signs and Seals

The sacraments are also, in the words of the Westminster Confession of Faith, "holy signs and seals of the covenant of grace, immediately instituted by God, to represent Christ, and his benefits; and to confirm our interest in him: as also, to put a visible difference between those that belong unto the church, and the rest of the world; and solemnly to engage them to the service of God in Christ, according to his Word."[12] Let's take these one at a time.

A *sign* points to something else. The sacraments serve as signs along the Christian road. They direct our attention to the life, death, and resurrection of Christ, who is Himself the way, the truth, and the life (see John 14:6). He is the narrow gate (see Matt. 7:13). He is the door (see John 10:9). Whenever we observe or meditate on these sacred signs—baptism and communion—we are directed again to see our hope in Christ.

The sacraments also function as seals. In past eras, royal figures were known by their seals, which were pressed into hot wax by a signet ring or other tool. Embossed on documents and possessions, the royal emblem communicated the mark of ownership and approval. The ordinances of the church serve as official seals that signify God's acceptance of us into His covenant. Again, as we said in the point about them being testimonies, participation in the ordinances does not grant or merit favor with God—it merely provides a visible mark of

---

12. Westminster Confession of Faith, 27.1.

the mercy and grace that He has already bestowed on us in Christ alone.

As Memorials

Finally, both ordinances hold enriching memories for those of us who trust Christ and fight sin. They retell the wonderful gospel story that we have come to love by grace through faith. And by retelling the gospel time and again, we have multiple opportunities to refresh our grasp on the good news of Jesus. Jacob experienced a vivid dream through which the covenant God assured him of His presence and favor, as He had to his forefathers. Awakened from the dream, Jacob used the stone on which he slept to make a pillar that would mark the incredible promise God had made (see Gen. 28:18). In a way, the ordinances serve as pillars of remembrance, reminding us of God's past, present, and future faithfulness through His eternal good news.

The sacraments proclaim the gospel to us over and over. When we observe the baptism of a fellow believer, we are reminded of our own declared intention to follow Jesus Christ, forsake sin, and remain openly identified with Jesus and His people. Reflecting on the meaning of water baptism brings to mind again our union with Christ, through which the pollution of sin was removed by our new life; the forgiveness of our sins; and the many gospel blessings that are now ours.

And every time we share the Lord's Supper together, we are reminded of Christ's redeeming sacrifice for us. Through the bread and the wine, we look to the past and remember the sin-bearing death of Jesus for us. We don't believe that Christ is present in the elements, but we certainly do gain strength for the present by communing with Jesus Himself (and with our fellow believers). There is also a forward-looking perspective in the Supper, through which we anticipate the great wedding feast we will enjoy in the presence of the Lamb and with His people (see Rev. 19:7–10). For these very reasons, Jesus instructed His disciples, as often as they gathered around the bread and the cup, to do it in remembrance of Him (see Luke 22:19).

Through the sacraments, our hearts are drawn anew to dwell on Christ and His life-transforming grace. But it also bears repeating that the ordinances are not merely memorial observances. There is in them a real, vertical dimension by which God ministers to us as we worship and remember Him. When we engage with baptism and the Lord's Supper in these ways, our souls are actively refreshed by the present and mysterious work of His grace.

Getting Serious about Change

On pages 187–90 of Appendix A, I've provided more practical steps for putting these provisions to work in your life. Turn there now to get started.

Carson's Diehard Sin

Carson is known as a lone-ranger Christian. Although he enjoys friendship with a handful of believers from work and school, he is not active in a healthy local church. "My relationship with God is private, and my busy life doesn't have time for a church," he insists. Carson is faithful to read God's Word, spend time in prayer, and do his best to lead a good life, but his trouble with lust and pornography persists. Unknowingly, by neglecting the God-ordained resources of the local church, Carson has placed himself at a serious spiritual disadvantage. Without the ongoing care, accountability, and fellowship of a loving church under competent pastors—God's people committed to him, and he to them—Carson is an army of one.

10

Fighting Sin in the Community of Faith

The Church is . . . a sanctuary for sinners saved by Grace, who,
though they are saved, are still sinners and need all the help they
can derive from the sympathy and guidance of their fellow Believers.
CHARLES SPURGEON (1834–1892)

Florida is a wonderful place. The weather is tropical through most of the year, and, no matter where you live, beautiful beaches beckon nearby. Every morning an exquisite sunrise welcomes the day, and every night an original work of art is painted across the sky. Of all that I admired during the five years I lived in Florida, you'll be surprised to hear what was near the top of my list: the grass. Wherever I looked, my eyes were drawn to lush and pristine yardscapes carefully manicured by the horticultural elite.

The most popular species of grass in Florida is called St. Augustine grass—a beautiful ground cover with a durable thatch so tightly woven that weeds struggle to fit in. But properly caring for this grass is no easy task. Most of the seeds are infertile, so it is specially designed to grow as one interlocking organism.[1]

1. L. E. Trenholm, J. B. Unruh, and T.W. Shaddox, "St. Augustinegrass for Florida Lawns," University of Florida IFAS Extension, September 2017, http://edis.ifas.ufl.edu/lh010.

This has been for me a helpful picture of God's design for the church. Victory over daily sin—as well as all spiritual growth, for that matter—does not come as the result of our living as independent seeds. True spiritual growth happens in the context of Christian community—from walking together as one united group of people who have been knit together in love (see Col. 2:2). Lasting biblical change requires constant engagement with Christ and His provisions, including church fellowship. In this final chapter, we will explore fighting sin in the community of faith.

Fighting Sin in Community Does Not Come Naturally

Isolation came second nature to Ken, whose heart was regularly ruled by fears and anxieties. Fear of public situations drove him to hide away in his house, and shame led him to shut out helpful people from his life. Throughout most of his life, Ken believed that freedom from anxiety was not possible. But, as he took his sinful habit of fear seriously, he learned the importance of fighting sin in community, not in solitude. In the community of faith, Ken found hope and help, accountability and instruction, counsel and encouragement. Although it was a new and awkward experience, he began to draw close to his pastor and to other Christians, allowing them to help him overcome his fears, worries, and anxieties. Ken learned that change is a community project.

From the beginning, God's plan has been to save and sanctify a holy people—not just individual persons (see Titus 2:14). Because we are made for community, it follows that our growth in the Christian life will happen within the community of faith. However, under the curse of sin, fighting sin in community does not come naturally. When we face any particular sin problem, our natural tendency is to retreat from other people. Shame and despair provoke us to hide—but isolation is unwise. By God's design, we need community with other believers who can help us.

To reap the benefits that God has ordained within the community of faith, we must move against the grain. During seasons of particularly difficult sin struggles, we may feel as though everything in us is screaming, "Run away!" We must do the opposite. "Lone ranger" Christianity does not lead to meaningful progress in the faith. On the contrary, isolation from the larger body of Christ actually disconnects us from many of the provisions Christ gives to us through the community He died to redeem.

If you and I are to overcome destructive daily habits, then the strategic and biblical actions we take that are critical to fighting sin must happen within the Christian community. Let's start with a broad view of the church and move narrower.

Place Yourself Under the Authority of a Faithful Pastor

The idea of shepherding is a key metaphor used in Scripture to describe the church. Our Lord Jesus came to be our Good Shepherd. His sheep hear His voice, they follow Him, and He cares for them. In an incredible display of affection, the Shepherd lays down His life for His sheep (see John 10:11–18). Jesus then builds His church, establishing under-shepherds to keep watch over the souls of His sheep (see 1 Peter 5:2). The caring ministry of pastoral shepherds is depicted throughout the New Testament.

God also displayed His attention to spiritual shepherding in the Old Testament. The prophets of Israel were charged with faithful care of the people, and when the shepherds failed to fulfill their role, God spoke strongly against them (see Jer. 23:1). His high standard communicates to us the importance of placing ourselves under the care of faithful pastors.

God tasks pastors with a threefold care of the souls of His people: feeding, leading, and protecting them (see Ezek. 34).[2] Let's take a look at each of these.

Sheep Need Food

Through His victory over temptation, our true and faithful Shepherd taught us that "man shall not live on bread alone, but on every word that proceeds out of the mouth of God" (Matt. 4:4). God's life-giving words have been delivered to us on the pages of Scripture. The Bible is a primary provision for the fight against sin, and God has also graciously provided us with pastors who rightly divide the Word of truth.[3]

The apostle Paul charged his spiritual son to handle the Scriptures accurately so that he might be approved by God as an unashamed pastor (see 2 Tim. 2:15). Timothy was to preach the Word, in all seasons patiently correcting, exhorting, and encouraging the people of God (see 2 Tim. 4:2). Why would God inspire Paul with a strong concern for Timothy to minister the Word faithfully? His sheep needed to be fed. I hope that you are in a church where faithful pastors regularly feed you through the public and private ministries of Scripture (see Acts 20:20).

---

2. Timothy Z. Witmer, *The Shepherd Leader: Achieving Effective Shepherding in Your Church* (Phillipsburg, NJ: P&R, 2010), 20–21.

3. Arthur W. Pink's words richly express this point: "It is by doctrine (through the power of the Spirit) that believers are nourished and edified, and where doctrine is neglected, growth in grace and effective witnessing for Christ necessarily cease. How sad then that doctrine is now decried as 'unpractical' when, in fact, doctrine is the very base of the practical life" (Arthur W. Pink, *The Sovereignty of God* [1919; repr., Lafayette, IN: Sovereign Grace, 2002], 261).

Sheep Need Leadership

As a faithful pastor feeds the people with God's Word, he also leads them with God's Word. Pastor and author Mark Dever writes, "We need God's Word to be saved, but we also need it to continually challenge and shape us. His Word not only gives us life; it also gives us direction as it keeps molding and shaping us in the image of the God who is speaking to us."[4] Faithful, expositional preaching is a primary task in the church. But biblical sermons are not enough—they do not eliminate counseling needs. On the contrary, good preaching stirs counseling needs to the surface. Worthy pastors know not only what God's Word says to us but also how it applies to us.

Imagine that you are lost on a road trip in a barren land where there is no GPS, and you stop for directions at a little gas station. The counter clerk is friendly, but forgetful. Although he knows of the city that you want to reach, he can't remember which roads will safely lead to your destination. On a scale of one to ten, how helpful is this clerk? He is *zero* help.

Faithful pastors give biblical direction to our walk with Christ. They know the destination of maturity as well as the roads that will lead us there. Good pastors are more than passionate preachers; they are also competent counselors who wisely lead others to repent, believe, and obey. John Calvin points to the importance of private pastoral care: "It is not enough for a man who is a shepherd in the Church of God, to preach, and cast abroad the word into the air, we must have private admonitions also."[5] Such private and personal leadership in life is invaluable to the person who wants to kill sin.

4. Mark Dever, *Nine Marks of a Healthy Church*, new ed. (Wheaton: Crossway, 2004), 51.

5. Quoted in Ray Van Neste, "The Care of Souls: The Heart of the Reformation," *Themelios* 39, no. 1 (April 2014), 56, available online at http://themelios .thegospelcoalition.org/article/the-care-of-souls-the-heart-of-the-reformation.

Do you know any pastors who are able to counsel you with the Word of God? I encourage you to enlist their help in the fight against diehard sins. God uses faithful pastors to help us with these difficult, relentless problems of life.

Sheep Need Protection

During the Vietnam War, retreating soldiers laid deadly traps to slow the progress of enemy forces. Although Jesus Christ has secured the victory of our war with sin, the forces of this present darkness endanger our progress in the faith at every turn. The Christian life is a treacherous journey through a fallen world. Therefore, the author of Hebrews exhorts us to submit to our pastoral leaders, because they watch over our souls (see Heb. 13:17). Godly shepherds provide an important protection for our souls. Every day we are faced with the daunting opposition of the world, the flesh, and the devil. The fact that books like this exist—books about the difficulties and perils of sin—prove just how serious is our need for soul care.

Sin is deadly—it's pervasive, persistent, enslaving, and hard to kill. We need every advantage we can find in the fight against sin. Let us not underestimate the powerful advantage that is godly pastoral protection. Our pastors will pray for, exhort, encourage, confront, convict, and comfort us in the fray. But in order for them to do this well, we must move toward them and the community of faith. If we allow shame or despair over our remaining sin habits to nudge us away from or out of the body of Christ, we will be the worse for it. We simply cannot and should not fight these battles alone.

If you have not already, please place yourself under the care of a faithful pastor or pastors in a healthy local church.[6] And

---

6. If you're not sure what kind of church to look for, I encourage you to read *Nine Marks of a Healthy Church* by Mark Dever.

if you already belong to a faithful church, continue to submit yourself to the feeding, leading, and protecting ministry of God's shepherds.

Commit Yourself to a Small Group of Christians in the Church

In the context of a healthy local church, under the loving oversight of competent pastors, you and I must remain connected to a small group of Christians. Regular attendance at the larger gatherings of the church is a nonnegotiable for the sin-fighting Christian—but some things cannot be accomplished in the corporate gathering of the local congregation. This includes small-group fellowship and accountability. We need a small group of our brothers and sisters who will watch out for us.

I am delighted to see how many churches are seriously pursuing small-group ministries. The small group to which I belong meets once per week. We share food, fellowship, prayer requests, and a time of down-to-earth discussion around our church's most recently preached sermon. In a small-group setting like this, we are able to discuss our trials and troubles more freely than we ever could during the larger Sunday-morning gathering. The ten to twelve people who attend my small group have become like family to me. We know one another, pray for each other, encourage one another, and counsel each other regularly.

Perhaps openly talking about temptation and sin, even in a small group, is a frightening thought for you. And indeed, sharing the more intimate details of our lives in Christ requires wisdom. But while transparency seems challenging at first, we soon realize just how many struggles we have in common with one another.

Paul pointed this out to the Corinthian believers when he wrote, "No temptation has overtaken you but such as is common to man" (1 Cor. 10:13). Without meaningful engagement with other Christians, we find ourselves thinking, *No one else struggles like I do. They all seem to be doing just fine.* These thoughts can drive us to isolation. But as we find courage to open up about our own destructive habits, the truth comes out: we are all a mess, and we need each other.

This not only means that you need other Christians in your life. It also means that other Christians need you. And here is an oft-forgotten reality. When we are in the throes of our own sin struggles, we lose sight of the mutual nature of church life. We think only about our own need for help in the fight against sin. But our brothers and sisters need us, too. Therefore, we ought to take small-group fellowship seriously—not just because we want to see our sin problems put to death, but because we want to see the sin problems of other people mortified as well.

You see, faithful and biblically-minded believers hate sin as far as the curse is found. We hate to see it in ourselves and in others. Our commitment to one another, and the understanding that our troubles are common to man, compel us to mutually care for all souls in the body of Christ. Commitment to a small group of believers is necessary for us to foster biblical love, promote fellowship, build the body, nurture our spiritual gifts, and kill sin.[7] What steps do you need to take in order to plant yourself among a small group of helpful fellow believers?

Connect Yourself to Personal Accountability

We have seen that the corporate gathering of believers is essential for those who contend valiantly with sin. And

---

7. See Neal F. McBride, *How to Lead Small Groups* (Colorado Springs: NavPress, 1990), 26–27.

commitment to a small group of believers will assist us even further in the battle. But even these efforts are often not strong enough to uproot most difficult and deceptive sin habits. An even tighter circle of help is needed in the fight. If you expect to make significant progress against destructive habits in your life, you must also submit yourself to personal accountability.

Those who you trust with the more intimate details of your life will have a clear path to enter your world, understand your need, and bring to you Christ and His provisions. You need one or two people who love you enough to stand by you, even while knowing everything about your diehard sin struggles. If you are a man, you need a couple of mature men who are willing to dig in with you as co-laborers. If you are a woman, you need a couple of mature women who are able to intimately care for you, and you for them. You need an inner circle to whom you will give a regular account of your successes, your failures, and everything in between.

Recognize that biblical accountability does not place on one person a responsibility for ferreting out the truth. It is not primarily one person digging up information about someone else; it is one person volunteering a truthful account of his life. Have you seen or been a part of an accountability relationship in which one person must constantly ask questions in order to find out how the other person is really doing? Biblical accountability is voluntary, and its sin-slaying power is activated through willful submission. You and I must willingly offer up the truth about our struggles to those who can help us make progress against our sin habits.[8]

Biblical accountability also is not a moralistic exercise

---

8. This is not to say that personal accountability requires no questions. It does. How else might someone enter our world and understand our need? Your willingness to divulge the details of your battles with diehard sins will provoke all kinds of questions.

for absolving our guilt. Confessional-booth accountability devolves into a system of sinning, confessing, and then sinning again. Only Christ, by His grace, can free our troubled souls.

In true personal ministry, people aim to shepherd one another with the truth and grace of Christ. People who are committed to biblical accountability strive to walk together, in mutual care, toward Christlikeness.[9]

Lord willing, a combination of voluntary accountability and wisely probing questions will lead you to life-changing answers from God's Word. Accountability provides another avenue for Christ and His answers to strengthen, comfort, and change you. If you could use stronger accountability in your life, act now. Ask your pastor to help you begin meeting weekly with one or two trusted people who can walk with you as they help you to deal seriously with whatever destructive habits are troubling you.

My prayer is for growth and maturity not only for us, but also for our churches. Jesus lived, died, and rose again for His Bride, and He is building His church into a vast, living testimony to His grace and glory. As a people of redeemed sinners who are knit together in love, the church is the central place in which God has ordained the slow, progressive death of sin. We must learn to fight sin together, under the care of our faithful shepherds, in community together, as we fight for the redemptive good of one another.

9. One pastor holds out a threefold purpose for accountability: identification of personal patterns of sin, mortification of sin through ongoing repentance, and sanctification through a united pursuit of holiness (see Jonathan Dodson, "Accountability Groups," *The Journal of Biblical Counseling* 24, no. 2 [Spring 2006]: 50–51).

Reflections for the Fight

1. In what ways can you draw near to others for the purpose of killing sin?
2. List some of the ways that your pastor or pastors spiritually feed, lead, and protect your soul.
3. How transparent are you willing to be about your struggle with persistent sin habits?
4. Are you currently accountable to one or more people who love you and help you in your walk with Christ? How can you be an encouragement to them?
5. Spend time right now talking to God about your need for change. Ask Him to give you grace, endurance, and anything else that you need to fight wisely against destructive daily habits.

Deidra's Diehard Sin

The suffocating weight of her loss was overwhelming just a year ago. After the sudden death of her friend, Deidra gave in to despair and gave up on life. She refused to believe in life after loss. Bitterness sprouted up from her heart, choking out any hope of happiness and joy. How could she ever move forward? Then grace broke through. As faithful brothers and sisters walked alongside her, Deidra set her eyes anew on Christ, who changes hearts and lives. One step of repentance after another led Deidra up and out of her hopelessness, as her clouds of disbelief gave way to the bright rays of the sun.

CONCLUSION

Moving Forward Together

In all your course, walk with God and
follow Christ as a little, poor, helpless child.
JONATHAN EDWARDS (1703–1758)

The Monster at the End of This Book was my favorite child-hood story. Are you familiar with it? Lovable, furry old Grover—a blue Muppet—is panic-stricken at the thought of facing a monster that waits for him at the end of the book. Every time a page turns, his desperation rises. Using bricks and ropes and wood and nails, he builds a series of obstacles to prevent the next page from advancing, but he is powerless. His angst is relieved when he learns that the only monster at the end of the book is him: lovable, furry old Grover. For a kid, the plot and conclusion were innocent and clever.

But now, through the lens of wisdom, I see how radically better is the redemptive story of Christ—a story in which the sovereign, wise, and good God reigns and rules, convicts and comforts, secures and sustains us on every page of the story that He has written for us. Our lives, with their hopes, dreams, fears, and regrets, are not about us, and our happy ending does not depend on a future lovable version of ourselves who waits for us to turn the last page. And we do not need to live in panic and desperation.

In the midst of our ongoing sin struggles, panic may well up in our hearts. In those times, we find assurance in knowing that the eternal covenant God of the gospel, who is full of saving, transforming, and enabling grace, accompanies us through every trouble, trial, and temptation. We can say with David, "Surely goodness and lovingkindness will follow me all the days of my life, and I will dwell in the house of the LORD forever" (Ps. 23:6).

My Only Regret

Unless you're a member of my little Midwestern church, we will probably never meet in person. I wish I could know your story: where you have been, what you are facing, where you'll end up. How wonderful it would be to sit for a while and share life together! While the details of our stories would differ, the parts that matter most would be quite similar. We are both sinners living in a fallen world, with the curse of sin at our backs, who are in need of future grace to comfort, confront, and change us.

Since meeting together for lunch is unlikely, I chose to sprinkle this book with the next best thing. Along the way, we've considered twelve different vignettes that represent all of us. The circumstances surrounding Janet's feelings of guilt or Carl's lazy ways or Melody's contentious relationships or Frank's doubts of God are varicolored and unique to each personal story. But in terms of what matters most, on the level of root and fruit, they are all the same. Like you and me, these people's sinful behavior, and the sinful hearts that drive their behavior, need to change. By recalling their stories throughout the book, we have made these twelve diehard sinners into examples of how the stream of God's gracious provisions in Christ helps us to repent, believe, and obey.

As you turn the final pages of this conclusion, you may look across the story line of your life and doubt whether things can change. But there is abundant hope, because God and His abounding grace are at the end of this book. I pray that you will know this.

No matter how entrenched your destructive daily habits have become, you can change. Change may not come as quickly as you would like or with a level of ease that you prefer, but change is promised in Christ. We, the people of God, are all moving forward together, at different speeds and in different ways. You are not alone. Together, God's people are marching toward a day of complete renewal; and, with each passing day, His grace will be sufficient to the very end. Pastor John Piper gives this important reminder:

> The only life I have left to live is future life. The past is not in my hands to offer or alter. It is gone. Not even God will change the past. All the expectations of God are future expectations. All the possibilities of faith and love are future possibilities. And all the power that touches me with help to live in love is future power. As precious as the bygone blessings of God may be, if He leaves me only with the memory of those, and not with the promise of more, I will be undone. My hope for future goodness and future glory is future grace.[1]

God is working all things for good to those whom He has lovingly called out of the darkness and into His eternal kingdom. Equipped with a more thorough understanding of sin's DNA, we are able to fight wisely against destructive daily

1. John Piper, *Future Grace: The Purifying Power of the Promises of God*, rev. ed. (Colorado Springs: Multnomah, 2012), 63.

habits. Because of God's past promises, immediate presence, and future grace, we can enter with joy into our daily struggles with sin. His revealed truth and the illuminating power of the Holy Spirit help us to understand our true needs and to make a proper diagnosis. Although on this side of eternity sin will remain a persistent problem, there is hope and help in Christ, who is ever at work for the glory of the Father and the good of His people.

My Future Hope for You

I hope that after reading this book you are better equipped to enter with joy into your daily struggle with sin, to understand your most important spiritual needs, and to bring Christ and His provisions to bear on the destructive daily habits that we all face as fallen people. I so wish that I could know you personally and see firsthand how God will continue His work in your life. I wonder what the next chapter in your story will be and how you will put into practice what we've considered in these pages. My prayer and challenge for all of us who wish to fight the good fight in the community of faith is merely an echo of Paul's desire for the believers of his day:

> That their hearts may be encouraged, having been knit together in love, and attaining to all the wealth that comes from the full assurance of understanding, resulting in a true knowledge of God's mystery, that is, Christ Himself, in whom are hidden all the treasures of wisdom and knowledge. I say this so that no one will delude you with persuasive argument. For even though I am absent in body, nevertheless I am with you in spirit, rejoicing to see your good discipline and the stability of your faith in Christ. Therefore as you have received Christ Jesus the Lord, so walk in Him, having been

firmly rooted and now being built up in Him and established in your faith, just as you were instructed, and overflowing with gratitude. (Col. 2:2–7)

By grace, we will keep up the fight together. Our final redemption is just over the horizon.

APPENDIX A

Putting God's Provisions to Daily Use

Action is an essential part of killing sin. We must become doers of the Word, which means putting into practice the biblical principles we have learned. Once you have read through chapters 8 and 9, use the following questions and exercises to equip you in your fight every day. Start today! Take it slow, and begin now to follow the instructions below. They will lead you into a more practical approach to fighting wisely against destructive daily habits.

The Provision of God Himself

Application: Extending Roots

- Focus on relating to God as your very present help in times of trouble. Regularly talk to God about His nearness. He is not far away, even as your fight with sin rages.
- Expand your knowledge of God's works, attributes, and promises by looking carefully for them in the Bible. Meditate on them in light of your diehard sin struggles.

- Your ongoing sin habits reveal what you actually believe about God and His ways. Through your growing knowledge of God in the Bible, compare what you believe to be true with what He has revealed to be true.

Application: Bearing Fruits

- Your heavenly Father, in Christ, promises His Spirit to be present with you and at work for your good. Throughout the day, thank God for His sovereign care of your life during times of spiritual difficulty.
- When you identify any rogue desire in your heart that is driving your diehard sin habit, immediately confess it to God. Entrust these ruling desires to Him, as though you are actually placing them in His loving hand.
- Knowing that you daily live before the face of God, make your highest treasure God's glory and pleasure. A desire to please God by grace will motivate you to kill your sin.

Recommended Reading

Knowing God by J. I. Packer
The Holiness of God by R.C. Sproul

The Provision of the Bible

Application: Extending Roots

- Evaluate your level of engagement with the Bible. What desires compete with your desire for God's Word?
- Psalm 19 describes God's words as being sweeter than honey. Confess to God ways in which you have lost a taste for His Word.

- Discern why your commitment to the Bible drops from time to time. Make a list of excuses that you use to justify the neglect of your scriptural nourishment.

Application: Bearing Fruits

- Allow the thoughts, words, and actions of Jesus, as recorded in the Scriptures, to direct your thoughts, words, and actions. How can the fruits of your daily life reflect the fruits that you see in Christ?
- Keep a journal of Scripture passages that speak directly to your particular diehard sin habits. In the moment of temptation or weakness, keep the journal as a ready tool to help you act on God's instructions.
- As you read Scripture, look specifically for the biblical dynamic of putting off sin and putting on righteousness.

Recommended Reading

Cross Talk by Mike Emlet
Praying the Bible by Donald Whitney

The Provision of the Gospel

Application: Extending Roots

- Open the Scriptures daily with the expressed purpose of knowing the gospel better. Note the ways you have understood or misunderstood the gospel before now.
- Behold the power, humility, and sacrifice of Jesus in the gospel. As you engage with Jesus in the good news, your beliefs will be conformed to the truth.
- Treasuring Christ in your heart, through frequent reminders of the gospel, will kill the sinful desires that aim to dethrone Him from your heart.

Application: Bearing Fruits

- With faith in the gospel, acknowledge your failures to God. Even when you are not under conviction, express to God the reality that you haven't loved Him or others as you should.
- Throughout each day, make it a habit to think about the gospel. For instance, take one aspect of Christ's redemptive work and hold it in your mind until you become familiar with it.
- Make it your aim to relate to other people in ways that are informed by the gospel. As God has graciously served you, seek to minister His grace to others.

Recommended Reading

The Gospel-driven Life by Michael Horton
The Gospel for Real Life by Jerry Bridges

The Provision of the Church

Application: Extending Roots

- Evaluate your current participation in church life. Are you involved in a healthy church where people honestly pray for, encourage, and counsel one another with the truth?
- Commit with another close friend to help each other fight against destructive daily habits. This commitment requires honesty about the true beliefs and desires of your hearts, as well as a willingness to speak and hear the truth.
- Carve out time to think of ways you will stir your fellow believers to a stronger sin-fighting brotherhood in your church.

Application: Bearing Fruits

- Enlist a small, tight circle of believers who will pray for your fight against sin, and vice versa.
- When you find yourself struggling with a particular sin, seek out a wise Christian or pastor who can give godly counsel and encouragement.
- Submit yourself to a faithful pastor who will guide you to replace the bad fruits of sin with the good fruits of the Spirit.

Recommended Reading

What Is a Healthy Church Member? by Thabiti Anyabwile
Speaking Truth in Love by David Powlison

The Provision of the Ordinances

Application: Extending Roots

- In your time alone with God, prayerfully reflect on the ordinances as provisions of God's grace that are brought into your life by the sacrificial love of Christ. Think about the meaning of baptism and communion and how they remind you of God's loving care for you.
- Meditate on Jesus's joyful sacrifice on the cross. Allow the beauty of His humility to work in you a longing to sacrifice your desires in exchange for His.
- As sin and temptation remain a part of your life, cling to a right belief in Jesus's finished work, His present care, and His promise to progressively change you until He comes again.

Application: Bearing Fruits

- When you take the Lord's Supper, thank God for sending Christ and ask Him to help you to live in the light of His good news. The Lord's Supper is an opportunity to examine your life and submit yourself to God's plan of change.

- Before you attend a baptism or communion service, prepare your heart to engage with the ordinances as testimonies, signs and seals, and memorials of your security in Christ.

- Day by day, make it your aim to anticipate the return of Christ and the wedding feast to follow. You can fight your present sin habits by looking forward to the coming of Christ's kingdom, in which sin will be finally killed.

Recommended Reading

Hungry by Rondi Lauterbach

How the Gospel Brings Us All the Way Home by Derek Thomas

APPENDIX B

Refuse—Replace—Pray—Praise

As children of the King, we can and must resist the temptation to sin. A simple four-letter acronym has helped me and others immensely to fight the allures of temptation: RRPP. Every time you face temptation to sin, use this tool to focus your heart on pleasing God by killing sin before it starts.

Refuse the Temptation in Jesus's Name

The character and power of Jesus motivate and enable His sons and daughters to say no to temptation. At the first whisper of our flesh, you and I need to be ready to refuse any sinful desire. Immediately talk to your rebellious heart: *No—Jesus is better! He has redeemed me from the pit and pulled me from my misery. How can I dishonor Him?* Say with Polycarp, a disciple of John who was threatened with a fiery death unless he betrayed Jesus, "For eighty and six years have I been his servant, and he has done me no wrong, and how can I blaspheme my King who saved me?"[1] Refuse temptation in Jesus's name!

---

1. Kirsopp Lake, trans., *The Apostolic Fathers* (New York: Putnam, 1917), 2:325.

Replace the Temptation with Scripture

The armor that God issues to His soldiers includes a two-edged sword. The Word of God is a powerful weapon in the fight against temptation. Yet, for many of us, our Bibles are too thin; our blades are dull. Let us feast on God's Word so that we will be ready to fight against sin with Scripture. When temptation looms, search the Word of God for a verse or passage that will call you away. Sin crouches at the door—drive it away, in the earliest moments of temptation, by actively engaging in the fight according to God's Word. Replace temptation with Scripture!

Pray the Other Way

As key Scriptures call your heart up and away from the grip of temptation, cry out to God for help. Pray toward the window of escape. When tempted toward impurity, pray toward holiness. When tempted with rage, pray toward gentleness and patience. When tempted to fear, pray toward confidence in God's sovereign care. Pray for God to deliver a special supply of fruits from His storehouse to strengthen you against temptation's assault. English Puritan Thomas Manton wrote, "One good way to get comfort, is to plead the promise to God in prayer . . . show him his handwriting; God is tender of his word."[2] Pray the other way!

Praise God for His Victory

God has given us a serious responsibility in the fight against sin and temptation. But His role is far greater. He supplies us

2. Thomas Manton, *One Hundred and Ninety Sermons on the Hundred and Nineteenth Psalm*, 3rd ed. (London, 1845), 1:223.

with the weapons of our war and the strength to fight the good fight. When sin and temptation flee or fall on the battlefield, our highest praise is due Him. As you experience a measure of success in pushing back against the curse of sin, lift your head to see who has ordained and secured your rescue. Praise God for His victory!

APPENDIX C

The PEAR Method

You may have heard the insightful proverb, attributed to Benjamin Franklin, "If you fail to plan, you are planning to fail." His modern-sounding proverb applies to nearly every endeavor, and it certainly applies to the Christian life. Without a clear, effective, and biblical plan for our spiritual growth, we put ourselves at a mournful disadvantage.

The good news is that our God is the ultimate planner, and He has given us everything pertaining to life and godliness (see 2 Peter 1:3). Here is a helpful plan, based on God's revealed wisdom, for how you can bring Christ and His truth into every situation. The acronym PEAR makes for easy recall. Plant its truth in your heart so that it will bear fruit.

Pray for Truth

Applying the Word of God to our lives requires first and foremost a dependence on God's help. Therefore, as our first instinct, we should beseech the Lord for grace to hear, receive, and know the truth. The rich gospel truths we need most are attainable only through His kind mercy, as He enlightens our minds with His revelation. While He has generally revealed Himself to the entire world, we long to know Him in a special way. We do not presume on His mercy, but we humbly submit ourselves to Him, praying for Him to sanctify us in the truth (see John 17:17).

Explore Truth

According to the grace God gives us in the truth, we then must set our minds on exploring the truth. Like a spelunker surveying a deep cavern, negotiating each pitch and squeeze, nook and cranny, corridor and crevice, the wise Christian will dive into the truth of God's Word. Our growing skills for Bible reading, meditation, memorization, and study flow beautifully into our serious quest to know God's revealed will. Intentionally apply yourself as an explorer of truth, feeding your insatiable appetite for spiritual discovery and change.

Act on Truth

We must not be content merely to explore and dig for truth. Important steps of action are required if the truths that we mine from Scripture are actually to set us free. James warns in his letter,

> If anyone is a hearer of the word and not a doer, he is like a man who looks at his natural face in a mirror; for once he has looked at himself and gone away, he has immediately forgotten what kind of person he was. But one who looks intently at the perfect law, the law of liberty, and abides by it, not having become a forgetful hearer but an effectual doer, this man will be blessed in what he does. (James 1:23–25)

Do you desire God's blessing in what you do? Then take action. Our common sin habits do not respond to mere knowledge of the truth or good intentions for change. Decisive biblical actions are needed. As you explore the truth, ask yourself, "What is God calling me to do in response to this passage of Scripture?"

Rejoice in Truth

How sweet would it be for you and me to experience real change in our struggles with ongoing trials, troubles, and temptations? No matter what particular sin problems recur in your life, any progress toward resisting and killing them is cause for celebration. And because God has already revealed His sufficient truth through His Son and in His Word, our rejoicing can begin now. We can and we should rejoice every day—not on behalf of platitudes that everything will be okay, but because our eyes have been opened to the truth and because God's grace is enabling us to wrestle with sin knowing that He is presently in us, for us, and working His good purposes through us.

APPENDIX D

Quotations to Consider

Each chapter in this book begins with a quote that is rich in biblical truth. Eight different theologians or pastors helped to gear our hearts to understand and fight sin. Here you will find each of those quotes in its larger context. Let's listen carefully and at length to these men of old, as their words of wisdom ring true for us even today.

Introduction: A Destructive Daily Problem

> But living a just and holy life requires one to be capable of an objective and impartial evaluation of things; to love things, that is to say, in the right order, so that you do not love what is not to be loved, or fail to love what is to be loved, or have a greater love for what should be loved less, or an equal love for things that should be loved less or more, or a lesser or greater love for things that should be loved equally.
>
> —St. Augustine, *Teaching Christianity*, trans. Edmund Hill, ed. John E. Rotelle (New York: New City Press, 2014), 1.27–28

Chapter 1: The DNA of Sin

> Sins are many times hid from the godly man's eye, though he commits them, because he is not diligent and accurate

in making a search of himself, and in an impartial studying of his own ways. If any sin be hid, as Saul was behind the stuff, or as Rahab had hid the spies, unless a man be very careful to search, he shall think no sin is there where it is. Hence it is that the Scripture doth so often command that duty of *searching* and *trying*, of examining and communing with our hearts. Now what need were there of this duty, but that it is supposed many secret and subtle lusts lie lurking in our hearts, which we take no notice of? If then the godly would find out their hidden lusts, know the sins they not yet know, they must more impartially judge themselves; they must take time to survey and examine themselves; they must not in an overly and slight manner, but really and industriously look up and down as they would search for thieves; and they must again and again look into this dark corner, and that dark corner of their hearts, as the woman sought for the lost groat. This self-scrutiny and self-judging, this winnowing and sifting of ourselves, is the only way to see what is chaff and what is wheat, what is mere refuse and what is enduring.

—Anthony Burgess, quoted in Charles Spurgeon, *The Treasury of David,* vol. 1 (London, 1870), 330

Chapter 2: Hope for the Smoldering Cinder

This violence for Heaven is the grand business of our lives: what did we come into the world for else? we did not come hither only to eat and drink, and wear fine [clothes]; but the end of our living is, to be violent for the kingdom of glory. . . . God sends us into the world as a merchant sends his factor to trade for him beyond the seas. So God sends us hither to follow a spiritual trade, to serve him and save our souls. If we spend all our time . . . in dressing and pampering our bodies, or idle visits, we shall give but a sad account to God, when he shall send us a letter of summons by death, and bid us *give an account of our stewardship*. Were not he much to be blamed that should have a great deal of timber given him to build him a house, and he should cut out all this brave timber into chips? Just so is the case of many; God gives them precious time in which they are to provide for a kingdom, and they waste this time of life, and cut it out all into chips. Let this excite violence in the things of God; it is the main errand of our living here; shall we go out of the world and forget our errand?

—Thomas Watson, *The Christian Soldier, or Heaven Taken by Storm*, 2nd ed. (New York, 1810), 110

Chapter 3: The Art of Contented Discontent

Let us take heed that a spirit of faint heartedness, rising from the seeming difficulty and disgrace involved in God's good ways, does not provoke God to keep us out of heaven. We see here what we may look for from heaven. . . . Christ will not leave us till he has made us like himself, all glorious within and without, and presented us blameless before his Father (Jude 24).

What a comfort this is in our conflicts with our unruly hearts, that it shall not always be thus! Let us strive a little while, and we shall be happy for ever. Let us think when we are troubled with our sins that Christ has this in charge from his Father, that he shall not "quench the smoking flax" until he has subdued all.

—Richard Sibbes, *The Bruised Reed* (1630), available online from Monergism at https://www.monergism.com/bruised-reed-ebook

Chapter 4: The Joy-Filled Fight

But "we all with open face," freely, boldly, and cheerfully, look upon the glory of God in the gospel. The light of the gospel is an alluring and comforting light; the light of the law was dazzling and terrifying. . . .

The law had not power to convert, to change into its own likeness; but now the gospel, which is the ministry of the Spirit, it hath a transforming changing power, into the likeness of Christ whom it preacheth. "We are changed from glory to glory" [2 Cor. 3:18]. It is a gradual change, not all at once, but from glory to glory, from one degree of grace to another; for grace is here called glory. . . .

The ministry of the gospel hath the Spirit with it, whereby we are changed from the heart-root inwardly and thoroughly . . .

The happiness of man consists especially in two things: In communion with God, in conformity to God.

—Richard Sibbes, *The Excellency of the Gospel above the Law* (1639), available online from Monergism at https://www.monergism.com/excellency-gospel-above-law-ebook

Chapter 5: Practicing Sin Detection

When Satan cannot get a great sin in he will let a little one in, like the thief who goes and finds shutters all coated with iron and bolted inside. At last he sees a little window in a chamber. He cannot get in, so he puts a little boy in, that he may go round and open the back door. So the devil has always his little sins to carry about with him to go and open back doors for him! And we let one in and say, "O, it is only a little one." Yes, but how that little one becomes the ruin of the entire man!

—Charles Haddon Spurgeon, "A Divine Challenge!" (sermon, New Park Street Chapel, London, April 22, 1860), in *Spurgeon's Sermons*, vol. 6, *1860*, available online from Christian Classics Ethereal Library at https://www.ccel.org /ccel/spurgeon/sermons06.txt

Chapter 6: Who Rules Your Heart?

Extol and magnify God's mercy, who has adopted you into his family; who, of slaves, has made you sons; of heirs of hell, heirs of the promise. Adoption is a free gift. He gave them power, or dignity, to become the sons of God. As a thread of silver runs through a whole piece of work, so free grace runs through the whole privilege of adoption. Adoption is greater mercy than Adam had in paradise; he was a son by creation, but here is a further sonship by adoption. To make us thankful consider, in civil adoption there is some worth and excellence in the person to be adopted; but there was no worth in us, neither beauty, nor parentage, nor virtue; nothing in us to move God to bestow the prerogative of sonship upon us. We have enough in us to move God to correct us, but nothing to move him to adopt us, therefore exalt free grace; begin the work of angels here; bless him with your praises who has blessed you in making you his sons and daughters.

—Thomas Watson, *A Body of Divinity*, available online from Christian Classics Ethereal Library at https://www.ccel.org /ccel/watson/divinity.txt

Chapter 7: The Power of Beliefs and Desires

Let us not cease, then, to ply the only instrument of powerful and positive operation, to do away from you the love of the world. Let us try every legitimate method of finding access to your hearts for the love of him who is greater than the world.

For this purpose, let us, if possible, clear away that shroud of unbelief which so hides and darkens the face of the Deity. Let us insist on his claims to your affection—and whether in the shape of gratitude, or in the shape of esteem, let us never cease to affirm, that in the whole of that wondrous economy, the purpose of which is to reclaim a sinful world unto himself—he, the God of love, so sets himself forth in characters of endearment, that nought but faith, and nought but understanding, are wanting, on your part, to call forth the love of your hearts back again.

—Thomas Chalmers, "The Expulsive Power of a New Affection," in *The Works of Thomas Chalmers, D. D.* (Philadelphia, 1833), 385

Chapter 8: Opening the Vaults of Gospel Treasure

I consider myself as the most wretched of men, full of sores and corruption, and who has committed all sorts of crimes against his King; touched with a sensible regret I confess to Him all my wickedness, I ask His forgiveness, I abandon myself in His hands, that He may do what He pleases with me. This King, full of mercy and goodness, very far from chastising me, embraces me with love, makes me eat at His table, serves me with His own hands, gives me the key of His treasures; He converses and delights Himself with me incessantly, in a thousand and a thousand ways, and treats me in all respects as His favourite. It is thus I consider myself from time to time in His holy presence.

—Brother Lawrence, *The Practice of the Presence of God: The Best Rule of Holy Life* (1692), available online from Christian Classics Ethereal Library at https://www.ccel.org/ccel/lawrence/practice.txt

Chapter 9: Nourishing Our Souls

When the devil throws our sins up to us and declares that we deserve death and hell, we ought to speak thus: "I admit that I deserve death and hell. What of it? . . . For I know One who suffered and made satisfaction in my behalf. His name is Jesus Christ, the Son of God. Where he is, there I shall be also."

—MARTIN LUTHER, *Letters of Spiritual Counsel*, trans. and ed. Theodore G. Tappert (Vancouver, British Columbia: Regent College, 2003), 86–87

Chapter 10: Fighting Sin in the Community of Faith

As I have already said, the Church is faulty, but that is no excuse for your not joining it, if you are the Lord's. Nor need your own faults keep you back, for the Church is not an institution for perfect people, but a sanctuary for sinners saved by Grace, who, though they are saved, are still sinners and need all the help they can derive from the sympathy and guidance of their fellow Believers.

—CHARLES HADDON SPURGEON, "The Best Donation" (sermon, Metropolitan Tabernacle, London, April 5, 1891), in *Spurgeon's Sermons*, vol. 37, *1891*, available online from Christian Classics Ethereal Library at https://www.ccel.org/ccel/spurgeon/sermons37.txt

Conclusion: Moving Forward Together

In all your course, walk with God and follow Christ as a little, poor, helpless child, taking hold of Christ's hand, keeping your eye on the mark of the wounds on his hands and side. From these wounds came the blood that cleanses you from sin and hides your nakedness under the skirt of the white shining robe of his righteousness.

—JONATHAN EDWARDS, *Jonathan Edwards' Resolutions and Advice to Young Converts*, ed. Stephen J. Nichols (Phillipsburg, NJ: P&R Publishing, 2001), 35

New from P&R and the Biblical Counseling Coalition

ADDICTIVE HABITS

CHANGING FOR GOOD

31 DAY DEVOTIONALS FOR LIFE

DAVID R. DUNHAM

AFTER AN AFFAIR

PURSUING RESTORATION

31 DAY DEVOTIONALS FOR LIFE

MICHAEL SCOTT GEMBOLA

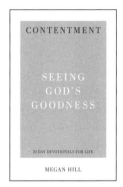

CONTENTMENT

SEEING GOD'S GOODNESS

31 DAY DEVOTIONALS FOR LIFE

MEGAN HILL

DOUBT

TRUSTING GOD'S PROMISES

31 DAY DEVOTIONALS FOR LIFE

ELYSE FITZPATRICK

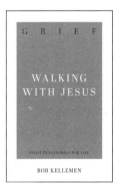

GRIEF

WALKING WITH JESUS

31 DAY DEVOTIONALS FOR LIFE

BOB KELLEMEN

PORNOGRAPHY

FIGHTING FOR PURITY

31 DAY DEVOTIONALS FOR LIFE

DEEPAK REJU

In the 31-Day Devotionals for Life series, biblical counselors and Bible teachers guide you through Scripture passages that speak to specific situations or struggles, helping you to apply God's Word to your life in practical ways day after day.

Devotionals endorsed by Brad Bigney, Kevin Carson, Mark Dever, John Freeman, Gloria Furman, Melissa Kruger, Mark Shaw, Winston Smith, Joni Eareckson Tada, Ed Welch, and more!

More from P&R on Law, Grace, and the Gospel

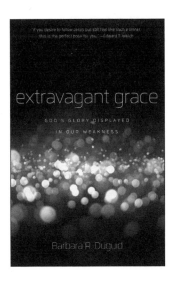

Why do Christians—even mature Christians—still sin so often? Why doesn't God set us free? Speaking from her own struggles, Barbara Duguid turns to the writings of John Newton to teach us God's purpose for our failure and guilt—and to help us adjust our expectations of ourselves. Rediscover how God's extravagant grace makes the gospel once again feel like the good news it truly is!

"Take this book to heart. It will sustain you for the long haul, long after the hyped-up panaceas and utopias fail."
   —**David Powlison**, Executive Director, Christian Counseling and Educational Foundation

"Buy this book. Buy one for a friend and live in the freedom that only the good news of the gospel can bring."
   —**Elyse Fitzpatrick**, Author, *Idols of the Heart*